Aristotle's Categories and
Propositions (De Interpretatione)

ARISTOTLE'S CATEGORIES AND PROPOSITIONS (DE INTERPRETATIONE)

Translated with Commentaries
and Glossary by
HIPPOCRATES G. APOSTLE

THOMAS MORE COLLEGE PRESS
Merrimack, New Hampshire

Copyright © 1980 by H. G. Apostle.

Copyright © 2021 by Thomas More College Press

Library of Congress catalog card number: 80-80777

Manufactured in the United States of America

ISBN 978-1-950071-04-3

To John M. Crossett

Contents

Preface

The *Categories* and the treatise *On Propositions* (*De Interpretatione*) are parts of the *Organon*, which is regarded as Aristotle's comprehensive treatment of logic and science. There is considerable evidence that the *Categories* was written earlier than the treatise *On Propositions* (as well as such works as *Physics*, *Metaphysics,* and *On the Soul*). The evidence is considered in several of my Commentaries on the *Categories*: Section 6, Comms. 4, 6, 7, 8; Section 8, Comm. 13; Section 10, Comms. 10, 12; Section 11, Comm. 1; Section 12, Comm. 4; Section 14, Comms. 1, 3, 4; and Section 15, Comm. 1. The treatise *On Propositions* was apparently written after the work *On the Soul*, judging from lines 16a8-9.

The principles used in the translation of the *Categories* and the treatise *On Propositions* are the same as those used in my translations of the *Metaphysics*, the *Physics*, and the *Ethics*. English terms common to all four translations have the same meaning, with a few exceptions, and the meanings of the key terms and the corresponding Greek terms are given in the Glossary. Some Greek terms, e.g., those translated as 'motion', 'quantity', and 'prior', do not have exactly the same meaning in the *Categories* as in the later works, and I have indicated in my Commentaries and the Glossary the changes in meaning. To distinguish in print an expression, whether vocal or written, from what it signifies, or of a thought from the object of thought, I enclose it in quotation marks. Since expressions in Greek are already distinguished typographically, they are not enclosed in quotation marks. Expressions appearing in brackets are added for the sake of clarity and are not translations from the Greek.

In the margins of the translation I have inserted the page and line numbers of the Bekker text, which are standard. Deviations from the Bekker text have been indicated and reasons for them have been given. The various works of Aristotle and the Bekker pages containing each of them are listed at the beginning of the Commentaries.

I am grateful to Professor John M. Crossett, who read the entire manuscript, made numerous corrections and suggestions, and clarified the meaning of certain terms which Aristotle uses in other works; to Professor Kretzmann, for a number of corrections; and to Grinnell College, for its assistance and encouragement.

H. G. A.

Grinnell College

I

Summary of the Categories

1. Definition of equivocal, univocal, and derivative names. 1a1-15.
2. (a) Composite and incomposite expressions. 1a16-19.
   (b) The said-of and present-in relations. 1a20-b9.
3. (a) Transitivity of predication. 1b10-15.
   (b) Different genera have different differentiae. 1b16-24.
4. List of categories; they are signified by incomposite names and are the highest genera. 1b25-2a10.
5. (a) Substances are either primary or secondary. Substances in the highest and most fundamental sense are primary and underlie all other things. 2a11-b6.
   (b) Species of substances are substances to a higher degree than their genera. 2b7-3a6.
   (c) No substance or differentia of a substance is present in anything. 3a7-32.
   (d) No name which signifies a substance is derivatively used. 3a33-b9.
   (e) A primary substance indicates a *this*, something which is an individual; a name of a secondary substance signifies not a primary substance but the quality or kind of a substance. 3b10-23.
   (f) No substance is contrary to another substance. 3b24-32.
   (g) No substance, *as such*, admits a variation of degree; but one kind of substance may be a substance to a higher degree than another kind, e.g., Socrates is a substance to a higher degree than man or animal. 3b33-4a9.
   (h) A substance, while remaining one and the same, has the property of admitting contraries, which are not substances. 4a10-b19.
6. (a) Quantities are either discrete or continuous. Numbers and speech are discrete quantities; lines, surfaces, bodies (or solids), time, and place are continuous quantities. 4b20-5a14.
   (b) In some quantities, the parts have relative position to each other; in others, the parts do not have relative position to each other. 5a15-37.

   (c) Things which are not quantities may be called 'quantities', but indirectly and not in the fundamental sense. 5a38-b10.

   (d) No quantity, *as such*, has a contrary. 5b10-6a18.

   (e) No quantity admits a variation of degree. 6a19-25.

   (f) Quantities have the property of being equal or unequal to each other. 6a26-35.

7. (a) The nature of relatives (or relations). 6a36-b14.

   (b) Relatives may be contraries. 6b15-19.

   (c) Relatives admit a variation of degree. 6b20-27.

   (d) Correlatives have reciprocal reference to each other. 6b28-7b14.

   (e) In most cases, correlatives exist at the same time. 7b15-8a12.

   (f) Are there any substances which are relatives? Some disagree in the case of secondary substances, but if a better statement of the nature of a relative is given, no substance can be a relative. 8a13-b24.

8. (a) One genus of qualities has habits and dispositions as its species. 8b25-9a13.

   (b) A second genus includes qualities which exist by virtue of a natural capability or incapability. 9a14-27.

   (c) A third genus includes affective qualities and affections as its species. 9a28-10a10.

   (d) A fourth genus of qualities is the shape or *form* of a thing. 10a11-26.

   (e) Things which are derivatively named according to quality are called 'such and such', e.g., 'brave' if they have bravery, which is a quality. 10a27-b11.

   (f) Qualities may be contrary to each other, e.g., justice and injustice, whiteness and blackness. 10b12-25.

   (g) Some things which are derivatively named according to quality admit a variation of degree. 10b26-11a14.

   (h) It is a property of qualities that things which are named according to them may be like or unlike. 11a15-19.

   (i) A problem arises whether some things may be relatives and also qualities. 11a20-38.

9. Acting and being acted upon admit contrariety and a variation of degree. As for the rest of the categories, no more need be said about them, for they are obvious. 11b1-14.

10. Things may be opposed in four ways: as relatives, as contraries, as privation and possession, and as contradictories; and all these oppositions are mutually exclusive. 11b15-13b35.

11. Some remarks about contraries. 13b36-14a25.

12. (a) In the most fundamental sense, A is said to be prior to B in time. 14a26-29.

(b) A is said to be prior to B if A exists when B exists, but the converse is not necessarily true. 14a29-35.

(c) A is said to be prior to B if A comes before B where there is some order. 14a36-b3.

(d) A is said to be prior to B if A is better or more honorable than B. 14b4-8.

(e) A is said to be prior to B if A is somehow a cause or the cause of B even if neither is prior to the other in existence. 14b9-23.

13. (a) In the most fundamental sense, A and B are said to be simultaneous if they come into being at the same time. 14b24-27.

   (b) A and B are simultaneous by nature if (i) both exist at the same time and neither is the cause of the existence of the other, or if (ii) they are immediate species or divisions of the same genus. 14b27-15a12.

14. (a) There are six kinds of motion: generation, destruction, increase, diminution, alteration, change of place; and all are distinct. 15a13-33.

   (b) Taken without qualification, the contrary of motion is rest; but in each kind of motion, the contrary of a motion may be a motion or may be rest. 15b1-16.

15. The word 'having' has many senses. 15b17-33.

Summary of On Propositions

1. The subject of this treatise is vocal expressions to which truth or falsity belongs, and their parts; and all such expressions are symbols or signs of mental impressions. 16a1-18.
2. Definition of a noun and an indefinite noun; cases of a noun or an indefinite noun. 16a19-b5.
3. Definition of a verb and an indefinite verb; tenses of a verb or an indefinite verb. 16b6-25.
4. Definition of a sentence. Only declarative sentences (i.e., propositions) will be considered in this treatise. 16b26-17a7.
5. A proposition is either simple, which may be an affirmation or a denial, or composed of simple propositions. Both affirmations and denials are said to be statements. Problems concerning what is simple and what is composite belong to another inquiry. 17a8-24.
6. The nature of an affirmation, a denial, and a contradiction (or contradictories). 17a25-37.
7. The subject of a statement may be universal or of an individual. Contrary and contradictory statements, and their relation to truth and falsity. 17a38-18a12.
8. Conditions under which a sentence is one statement or many statements. 18a13-27.
9. Relation of statements concerning future particulars to truth and falsity, and determinism. 18a28-19b4.
10. An analysis of the various kinds of opposite propositions and their relation to truth and falsity. 19b5-20b12.
11. Conditions under which (a) an expression, whether a noun or a verb, is one or many, and (b) names in related statements may be combined or analyzed. 20b13-21a33.
12. The manner in which statements concerning necessity, possibility, impossibility, and what may be should be formed to produce contradictories. Some remarks about necessary being and potential being. 21a34-22a13.
13. Relations between the various statements concerning possibility, impossibility, necessity, and what may be. 22a14-23a26.
14. The kinds of statements or opinions which should be regarded as being contrary. 23a27-24b9.

CATEGORIES

1

1a

Things are named equivocally[1] if only the name applied to them is common but the expression of the *substance* [i.e., the definition][2] corresponding to that name is different for each of the things, as in the case of a man and a picture[3] when each is called 'animal'. For only the name is common to these, but the expression of the *substance* corresponding to that

5 name differs for each; for if one were to state what it is to be an animal, he would give a different definition for each of them.[4]

Things are named univocally if both the name applied to them is common and the expression of the *substance* corresponding to that name is the same for each of the things, as in the case of 'animal' when applied to a man and to an ox. For a man and an ox may be called by the common

10 name 'animal', and the expression of the *substance* [corresponding to that name] is the same for both; for if one were to state for each of them what it is to be an animal, he would give the same definition.

Things are derivatively named if they are called by a name which is borrowed from another name but which differs from it in ending. For example, a man may be called 'grammarian', and this name is borrowed

15 from 'grammar'; and he may be called 'brave', and this name is borrowed from 'bravery'[5].

2

Of the expressions, some are composite but others are not composite. For example, 'man runs' and 'man conquers' are composite, but 'man', 'ox', 'runs', and 'conquers' are not composite.[1]

20 Of things, (1) some are said of a subject but are not present in any subject. For example, man is said of an individual man, which is the subject, but is not present in any subject. (2) Others are present in a subject but are not said of any subject (a thing is said to be present in a subject if, not belonging as

25 a part to that subject, it is incapable of existing apart from the subject in which it is). For example, a particular point of grammar is present in the soul[2], which is the subject, but is not said of any subject, and a particular whiteness is present in a body (for every color is in a body), which is the subject, but is not said of any subject. (3) Other things, again, are said of a

1

1b

subject and are also present in a subject. For example, *knowledge* is present in the soul, which is the subject, and is said of a subject, e.g., of grammar. Finally, (4) there are things which are neither present in a subject nor said

5

of a subject, such as an individual man and an individual horse; for, of things such as these, no one is either present in a subject or said of a subject. And without qualification, that which is an individual and numerically one is not said of any subject, but nothing prevents some of them from being present in a subject; for a particular point of grammar is present in a subject but is not said of any subject.[3]

3

10

When one thing is predicable of another as of a subject, whatever is said of the predicate will be said of the subject also. For example, 'man' is predicable of an individual man, and 'animal' of 'man' [or of man];

15

accordingly, 'animal' would be predicable of an individual man also, for an individual man is both a man and an animal.[1]

The differentiae of genera which are different and not subordinate one to the other are themselves different in kind, as in the case of 'animal' and 'science'. For the differentiae of 'animal' are 'terrestrial', 'two-footed', 'feathered', 'aquatic', etc., and none of these is a differentia of 'science'; for

20

no science differs from another by being two-footed[2]. But if one genus comes under another, nothing prevents both genera from having differentiae which are the same; for a higher genus is predicable of a genus coming under it, and so all the differentiae of the predicate [the higher genus] will be differentiae of the subject [the lower genus] also.[3]

4

25

Expressions which are in no way composite signify[1] either a substance, or a quantity, or a quality, or a relation,[2] or somewhere, or at some time, or being in a position,[3] or possessing [or having], or acting, or being acted upon. To speak sketchily, examples of a [name signifying a] substance are 'a man' and 'a horse'; of a quantity, 'a line two cubits long' and 'a line three cubits long'[4]; of a quality, 'the white' and 'the grammatical'; of a relation, 'a

2a

double', 'a half', and 'the greater'; of somewhere, 'in the Lyceum' and 'in the Agora'; of at some time, 'yesterday' and 'last year'; of being in a position, 'lies' and 'sits'; of possessing, 'is shod' and 'is armed'; of acting, 'cuts' and 'burns'; of being acted upon, 'is cut' and 'is burned'.[5]

5

Each of the above, when by itself, is not expressed as an affirmation or a denial, but an affirmation or a denial is formed only if such expressions are

combined; for every affirmation and every denial is thought to be either true
10   or false, whereas no expression which is in no way composite, such as 'a man'
or 'white' or 'runs' or 'conquers', is either true or false.[6]

5

A substance, spoken of in the most fundamental, primary, and highest
sense of the word is that which is neither said of a subject nor present in a
subject;[1] e.g., an individual man or an individual horse. Secondary
substances are said to be (a) those to which, as species, belong substances
15   which are called 'primary', and also (b) the genera of those species. For
example, an individual man comes under the species man, and the genus of
this species is animal; so both man and animal are said to be secondary
substances.[2]
20   It is evident from what has been said that, of things said of a subject, it
is necessary for both the name and the definition [corresponding to that
name] to be predicable of that subject. For example, man is said of an
individual man, which is a subject; so the name 'man', too, is predicable [of
the individual man], for one would predicate 'man' of an individual man.
25   And the definition of man, too, would be predicable of the individual man;
for an individual man is a man and also an animal.[3] Thus both the name and
the corresponding definition would be predicable of the subject.
Of things which are present in a subject, in most cases neither the name
nor the definition corresponding to that name is predicable of the subject.
30   In some cases, however, sometimes nothing prevents the name from being
predicable of the subject, but the definition [corresponding to that name]
cannot be predicable of that subject. For example, white is present in a
body, which is the subject, and [the name 'white'][4] is predicable of that
subject (for that body is called 'white'); but the definition of white will never
be predicable of that body.[5]
35   Everything except primary substances is either said of a subject which is
a primary substance or is present in a subject which is a primary substance;
and this becomes evident if particular cases are taken. For example, 'animal'
is predicable of man,[6] and hence it would be predicable of an individual
2b   man also; for if it were not predicable of any individual man, neither would
it be predicable of man at all. Again, color is present in body, and hence it
would be present in an individual body also; for if it were not present in any
individual body, neither would it be present in body at all. Thus everything
5   except primary substances is either said of a subject which is a primary
substance or is present in a subject which is a primary substance.
Accordingly, if primary substances did not exist, it would be impossible for
any of the others to exist.[7]

Of secondary substances, the species is to a higher degree a substance than a genus of it, for it is closer to a primary substance than a genus of it is. For if one were to state what a given primary substance is, he would give something which is more informative and more appropriate to that substance by stating its species than by stating a genus of it.[8] Of an individual man, for example, he would give more information by calling him 'man' than by calling him 'animal'; for the name 'man' is more proper to the individual man than the name 'animal', whereas the name 'animal' is more common than 'man'. Again, in the case of an individual tree, he will give more information by calling it 'tree' than by calling it 'plant'.

Moreover, primary substances are said to be substances in the highest degree because they underlie all the rest and all the rest are either predicable of or present in primary substances. Now the relation of primary substances to all the rest is similar to that of a species [of a primary substance] to a genus of it, since the species underlies the genus; for a genus is predicable of a species of it, whereas a species is not predicable of a genus of it. So in view of this, too, a species [of a primary substance] is a substance to a higher degree than a genus of it. But of the species themselves which are not genera of lower species, no one of them is a substance to a high degree than another; for you will not give a more appropriate account of the subject by calling an individual· man 'man' than by calling an individual horse 'horse'. And in a similar way, of primary substances, no one of them is a substance to a higher degree than another; for an individual man is not a substance to a higher degree than an individual ox.

Of all things other than primary substances, it is reasonable that only the species and the genera [of primary substances] should be called 'secondary substances', for of all the predicates these alone [as predicates] indicate a primary substance. For, if one is to state what an individual man is, it is by stating the species or a genus of it that he will say something which is appropriate to him, and he will give more information by saying that he is a man than by saying that he is an animal. Anything else that he might say of him, e.g., that he is white or that he runs or any other such thing, would be remote from him.[9] Thus it is reasonable that, of all things other than primary substances, only the species and the genera [of primary substances] should be called 'substances'.

Moreover, it is because they underlie all other things that primary substances are called 'substances' in the most fundamental sense. In fact, just as primary substances are [thus] related to all other things, so the species and genera of primary substances are related to all other things [except primary substances], for all these are predicable[10] of those species and genera. Thus if we call an individual man 'grammatical', this predicate will apply also to [the species] man and to [the genus] animal; and similarly with all other cases.

It is common to all substances that none of them is present in a subject. For a primary substance is neither present in a subject nor said of a subject; and as for secondary substances, it is evident from what follows also that they are not present in a subject. For man is said of an individual man, who is the subject, but is not present in a subject; for man is not present in an individual man. Similarly, animal, too, is said of an individual man, who is the subject, but animal is not present in an individual man.[11] Again, of a thing present in a subject, sometimes nothing prevents the name [of that thing] from being predicable of the subject in which the thing is present, but the corresponding definition of the thing cannot be predicable of that subject. Of a secondary substance, on the other hand, both the name and the definition are predicable of the corresponding subject; for we would predicate of an individual man both the definition of man and that of animal.[12] Thus a substance is not a thing which is present in a subject.

Now this fact is not a property of substances since the differentia [of a substance], too, is not present in a subject; for terrestrial and two-footed are said of man, who is the subject, but are not present in a subject, for they are not present in man. The definition of a differentia, too, is predicable of that of which the differentia is said; for example, if terrestrial is said of man, the definition of terrestrial will be predicable of man also, for man is terrestrial.[13]

Let us not be confused by the thought that the parts of a substance are in the whole substance as if present in a subject and be forced to say that those parts are not substances; for we said earlier that by 'being present in a subject' we do not mean existing as parts[14] which belong to some whole.

It is a mark of substances and [their] differentiae that all things are univocally named from them;[15] for all the predicates corresponding to them are predicable either of individuals or of species. First, since a primary substance is not said of a subject, the corresponding predicate cannot be predicable of anything.[16] As for secondary substances, the species is predicable of the individuals, and the genus is predicable both of the species and of the individuals. The differentiae [of substances], too, are likewise predicable of the species as well as of the individuals. Again, primary substances admit of the definition of their species and the definition of their genera, and a species [of a substance] admits of the definition of its genus; for whatever is said[17] of the predicate will be said[17] of the subject also. Similarly, both the species and the individuals admit of the definition of the differentia. But things were stated to be univocally named if both the name is common and the definition corresponding to that name is the same; hence all things are univocally named from a substance or a differentia [of a substance].

Every substance is thought to indicate a *this*.[18] Now in the case of primary substances there is no dispute, and it is true that a primary substance indicates a *this*; for what is exhibited is something individual and numerically one. But in the case of a secondary substance, though the manner of naming it appears to signify in a similar way a *this*, as when one uses 'a man' or 'an animal',[19] this is not true, for [such a name] signifies rather a sort of quality; for the subject is not just one [in an unqualified way], as in the case of a primary substance, but man or animal is said of many things. Nevertheless, such a [name] does not signify simply a quality, as 'white' does; for 'white' signifies a quality and nothing more, whereas a species or a genus [of a primary substance] determines the quality of a substance, for it signifies a substance which is qualified in some way. But the determination in the case of a genus is wider in application than that in the case of a species, for he who uses the name 'animal' includes more things than he who uses the name 'man'.

Another mark of a substance is that it has no contrary. For what would be the contrary of a primary substance, e.g., of an individual man or of an individual animal? There can be none. Nor can there be a contrary of man or of animal. This mark, however, is not a property of substances but is common to many other things also, for example, to quantities; for there can be no contrary to a line two cubits long or three cubits long, nor to the number ten, nor to any other such thing, though one might say that much is the contrary of little and that great is the contrary of small.[20] But of a definite quantity there can be no contrary.

Again, no substance is thought to admit of variation of degree.[21] By this I mean not that one [kind of] substance cannot be more of a substance or less of a substance than another (for it has already been stated that this is the case),[22] but that each substance, *as such*,[23] is not said to admit of variation of degree. For example, if that substance is a man, he cannot be more of a man or less of a man, whether he is compared with himself [at different times] or with another man; for one man is not more of a man than another man,[24] unlike one white thing which may be more white, or less white, than another white thing, or one beautiful thing which may be more beautiful, or less beautiful, than another beautiful thing. Now the same thing may admit of variation of degree [but with respect to quality]; a body which is white, for example, may be [truly] said to be more white now than before, and a body which is hot may be [truly] said to be more hot [at one time than at another]. But a substance [*as such*] is never [truly] said to vary in degree; for neither is a man [truly] said to be more of a man now than before, nor is this the case with any of the other [kinds of] substances. Accordingly, a substance [*as such*] does not admit of variation of degree.

The mark most proper to a substance is thought to be that, while remaining numerically one and the same, it admits of contraries.[25] In other words, of all things other than [primary] substances, there is no one which, being numerically one [and the same], can be shown to admit of contraries.

A color, for example, being numerically one and the same, cannot be black and white; nor can an *action*, which is numerically one and the same, be both vicious and virtuous; and similarly with other things which are not substances. But a substance, being numerically one and the same, admits of contraries.[26] An individual man, for example, being [numerically] one and the same, becomes at one time light but at another dark in color, at one time warm but at another cold, at one time vicious but at another virtuous.

No such thing appears to apply to any of the other things, although one might object and maintain that a statement or an opinion admits of contraries. For the same statement is thought to be [sometimes] true and [sometimes] false; for example, if the statement 'that man is sitting' is true, the same statement will be false after that man gets up. The same applies to opinions; for if one's opinion that a man is sitting is true, then the same opinion of the same man will be false after that man gets up. Yet even if we were to allow this to be so, still the manner in which it happens here differs from that in the other case; for in the other case it is by a change in themselves that substances admit of contraries, for it is by changing himself (i.e., by altering) that a man became warm from cold, or dark from light, or virtuous from vicious. It is likewise with the other substances, for it is by a change in itself that each of them admits of contraries. But in themselves, statements and opinions keep on being immovable in every way, and they admit of contraries only when the things [signified by them] have moved; for the statement 'that man is sitting' keeps on being the same in itself, but it is said to be first true and then false only when the thing [i.e., that man] has moved; and the same applies to opinions. Thus, at least in the manner indicated, only substances have the property of admitting of contraries in virtue of their own change. So if one accepts also these qualifications, then it would not be true to say that statements and opinions admit of contraries; for it is not by receiving any contraries in themselves that they are said to admit of contraries but by the fact that some other things [i.e., substances] have been affected in this manner, since a statement is now true and later false not by admitting in itself now one contrary and later another but because what is signified is a fact now but not later.[27] In fact, neither a statement nor an opinion can be moved in an unqualified way[28] by anything, so they cannot admit of contraries if they cannot be affected. But as for substances, it is by receiving the contraries in themselves that they are said to admit of contraries; for [animals] become sick and healthy, light and dark, and they are said to admit of contraries when they themselves receive them. Accordingly, it is only a substance that, being the same and numerically one,[29] has the property of admitting contraries in virtue of its own change.

Let so much be said concerning substances.

6

Of quantities, some are discrete but others are continuous;[1] and some are composed of parts which have relative position to each other, others are composed of parts which do not have relative position to each other. Examples of a discrete quantity are a [whole] number[2] and speech; examples of a continuous quantity are a line, a surface, a body,[3] and, besides these, time and place.[4]

The parts of a number have no common boundary at which they join. For example, five as a part of ten is not joined with the other part, five, at any common boundary, but the two parts are discrete, and three, which is another part of ten, is not joined with the other part, seven, at any common boundary; and in general, it is not at all possible to find any boundary among the parts of a number, for those parts are always discrete. A number, then, is a discrete quantity.[5] Speech is likewise a discrete quantity. Evidently, speech is a quantity, for it is measured by short and long syllables; and by 'speech' here I mean vocal speech. Now the parts of speech have no common boundary at which they join, for there is no common boundary at which the syllables are joined; each syllable is separate by itself.[6]

A line, on the other hand, is a continuous quantity, for it is possible to find a common boundary — a point — at which its parts are joined; and in the case of a surface, the boundary is a line, for the parts of a plane are joined at some common boundary. Similarly, it is possible to find a common boundary — a line or a surface — at which the parts of a body are joined. Time and place, too, are quantities like these. For present time is joined with the past and also with the future.[7] Place, too, is continuous, for the parts of a body occupy a place and are thus joined at some common boundary; and so the parts of place, too, which the parts of the body occupy, are joined at the same boundary at which the parts of the body are joined. Hence place, too, would be continuous, for its parts are joined at a common boundary.[8]

Again, some quantities are composed of parts which have a relative position to each other, others are composed of parts without having a relative position to each other. For example, the parts of a line have a relative position to each other, for each part lies somewhere, and one could mark off each part and state where it lies in the plane and with which of its other parts it is joined.[9] Similarly, the parts of a plane have a [relative] position, for one could state in a similar way where each part lies and with which of the other parts it is joined. Similar remarks apply to a solid and to place.

But in the case of a number, one could not point out how its parts have a relative position to each other or lie somewhere, or which parts are joined with other parts. Nor could one do so in the case of time, for no part of time continues to exist; and how could a thing have position if it cannot continue

to exist? One would rather say that the parts of time have an order in which
any one part comes either before or after another. And similarly with
numbers, for, in counting, one comes before two, two before three, etc., and
in this way there would be an order;[10] but it would not be possible at all to
find any position. The same applies to speech also. None of its parts
continues to exist, and after it has been pronounced, it no longer exists; and
if the parts cannot continue to exist, they can have no position. Accordingly,
some quantities are composed of parts having a [relative] position, others are
composed of parts having no position.

Quantities in the fundamental sense are only those which we have
mentioned; all the others are called 'quantities' indirectly, for we call them
so because we have in mind some quantity in the fundamental sense. For
example, the white is called 'much' since the surface which is white is
much,[11] and an *action* is called 'long' since it takes much time, and a motion
is called 'extended' for the same reason; for each of these is so called not in
virtue of its nature. In other words, if one were to answer the question 'How
long did the *action* take?', he would specify it in terms of time and say that
it took one year, or something of the sort; and to the question 'How large is
the white?', he would specify the answer in terms of the surface, for he
would say that the white has so much surface. Thus quantities in the
fundamental sense and in virtue of their own nature are only the ones
mentioned; the others are not quantities in virtue of their nature but, if at
all, [are called 'quantities'] indirectly.

Again, there can be no contrary to a quantity. In the case of definite
quantities it is evident that there can be no contrary, e.g., to a line two or
three cubits long[12] or to a surface or to any such quantity; for there is no
contrary to any of these, although one might maintain that much is contrary
to little and that the great is contrary to the small. But these are relatives and
not quantities, for no thing in virtue of its nature is called 'great' or 'small',
but only when it is referred to some other thing. For example, a mountain
may be called 'small' but a grain 'large', and this is in view of the fact that
the latter is greater than others of its kind while the former is smaller than
others of its kind. Thus there is a reference to some other thing, for if these
were called 'small' or 'large' in view of their own nature [i.e., without being
referred to something else], the mountain would not be called 'small' and
the grain 'large'. Again, we say that there are many men in the village but
few men in Athens, although those in Athens are many times more than
those in the village; and we say that there are many people in the house but
few in the theatre, although those in the theatre are many more than those
in the house. Again, the expressions 'a line two cubits long' and 'a line three
cubits long' and others like them signify quantities; 'great' and 'small', on
the other hand, signify not quantities but rather relatives, for the great or
the small is viewed with reference to something else. So it is evident that
these [i.e., 'great', 'small', etc.] are relatives.[13]

30   Again, whether one posits the above as being quantities or not, still no thing can be contrary to each of them; for how can one [truly] maintain that there can be a contrary to a thing which is considered not in virtue of its nature but by being referred to something else?[14] Again, if the great and the small were contraries, the same thing would turn out (a) to admit of

35 contraries at the same time and (b) to be contrary to itself. (a) For sometimes the same thing happens to be great and small at the same time, small in relation to one thing but great in relation to another; and so the same thing would turn out to be both great and small at the same time and hence to

6a admit of contraries at the same time. Yet no thing is thought to admit of contraries at the same time, as in the case of substances. Although a man, for example, is thought to admit of contraries, still he cannot be both sick and healthy at the same time; nor can a body be both white and black at the same time. In fact, no thing at all admits of contraries at the same time.[15]

5 (b) And the same thing would turn out to be contrary to itself. For if the great were contrary to the small, since the same thing is both great and small at the same time, the same thing would be contrary to itself. But it is impossible for anything to be contrary to itself. Hence neither is the great

10 contrary to the small, nor is much contrary to little. So even if one were to call these 'quantities' and not 'relations', still they would have no contraries.[16]

    Contrariety in quantities is thought to belong to place most of all. For men posit up as being contrary to down, calling 'down' the space at the

15 center of the universe because its distance from the outer limits of the universe is the greatest. And they seem to apply this terminology to the definition of contraries for all other things, for they define contraries in a given genus as things whose distance from each other is the greatest.[17]

20   Quantities do not admit of variation of degree. For example, a line two cubits long is not more of a line or less of a line than another line two cubits long; and in the case of numbers, one instance of three is not more three than another instance of three, and one instance of five is not more five than another. And of time, too, one instance of it is not more time than another instance of it. In general, of the kinds of quantities mentioned, no one instance can be truly said to be more or to be less of what it is than another

25 instance. So quantities, too, do not admit of variation of degree.

    The most proper attribute of quantities is that they are said to be equal or unequal to each other, for in each of the kinds of quantities mentioned one quantity is said to be either equal or unequal to another. For example, one body is either equal or unequal to another, one interval of time is either

30 equal or unequal to another, and similarly for each of the other kinds of quantities mentioned.[18] Concerning things other than quantities, no one would ever think of saying that they are either equal or unequal. A disposition, for example, is certainly not said to be equal or unequal to

another disposition but rather similar, and one white thing is not said to be
equal or unequal to another white thing, but rather similar. So the most
35   proper attribute of a quantity is that it is [truly] said to be either equal or
unequal to some other quantity.

7

Things are called 'relative' [or 'relations']¹ if *as such*² they are said to be
of³ something else or to be somehow referred to something else. For
example, the greater, *as such*, is said to be of something else, for it is said
to be greater than some other thing, and the double, *as such*, is said to be
6b   of something else, for it is said to be double of some other thing. It is likewise
with all others of this sort. Other examples of relatives are the following:
possession, disposition, sensation, *knowledge*, and position⁴; for each of
these, *as such*, is said to be of something else and is not stated in any other
way. For a possession is said to be a possession of something, *knowledge* is
5   said to be *knowledge* of something, a position is said to be a position of
something, and similarly with all others.⁵ Accordingly, relatives are things
which, *as such*, are said to be of something else or are referred to something
else in some way or other. For example, a mountain is called 'great' when
it is related to something, for it is so called by being referred to something;
10   and that which is said to be similar is similar to some other thing, and all
others of this sort are said to be relative in the same way. Lying, standing,
and sitting, we may add, are positions, and position is a relative. But to lie,
to stand, and to be seated are not themselves positions; they are derivatively
so expressed from the corresponding positions.⁶
15   Contraries may exist among relatives. For example, virtue is contrary to
vice, and each is a relative; and *knowledge* is contrary to ignorance.⁷ But not
all relatives have contraries; for there is no contrary to a double, or to a
triple, or to any other such thing.
20   Relatives are thought to admit also of variation of degree. For a thing may
be said to be more similar, or less similar, or more dissimilar, or less
dissimilar [to something than to something else], or it may be said to be more
equal, or less equal, or more unequal, or less unequal [to something than to
something else], and each of these is a relative; for the similar is said to be
similar to something, and the dissimilar is said to be dissimilar to something.
25   But not all relatives admit of variation of degree; for the double is not said
to be more double or less double [to something than to something else], and
the same applies to other such things.⁸
All relatives have reciprocal reference to their correlatives. For example,
30   a slave is said to be the slave of a master, and a master is said to be the master

of a slave; a double is said to be the double of a half, and a half is said to be the half of a double; and the greater is said to be greater than the less, and the less is said to be less than the greater. It is likewise with the other relatives, except that sometimes the expression requires a different grammatical case. For example, *knowledge* is said to be *knowledge* of the *known*, but the *known* is said to be *known* by *knowledge*; and sensation is said to be sensation of the sensible, but the sensible is said to be sensible by sensation.[9]

Sometimes, however, no reciprocal reference is thought to arise if a relative is not appropriately but mistakenly rendered when referred to [its correlative]. For example, if a wing is stated as being the wing of a bird, no reciprocal reference arises, since a bird is not a bird of the wing; for 'the wing of a bird' is not the appropriate expression since the wing is said to be of a bird not insofar as the latter is a bird but insofar as it is winged, for there are many other things, too, which have wings but are not birds.[10] Thus if the expression is appropriately rendered, there is a reciprocal reference, e.g., a wing is a wing of the winged, and the winged is winged by the wing.

Sometimes it is perhaps necessary to introduce a new name, if no name exists to which a relative might be appropriately rendered. For example, if a rudder is stated to be of a boat, the statement is not made appropriately, for a rudder is said to be of a boat not insofar as the latter is a boat (for there are boats without rudders, and so there is no reciprocal reference) since a boat is not said to be the boat of [or by, etc.] a rudder. Perhaps the expression would be more appropriately rendered if one were to introduce a word such as 'ruddered', since no name exists, and to say that the rudder is a rudder of the ruddered, or something of this sort; and if the expression is appropriately rendered in this manner, the reference will be reciprocal, for the ruddered is ruddered by the rudder, and the same applies to others of this sort. To take another example, a head would be more appropriately rendered [as a relative] if it were stated to be of the headed rather than of an animal, for it is not insofar as it is an animal that an animal has a head—for many animals have no head—[but insofar as it is headed].

Perhaps the easiest way to grasp relatives which have no names is to posit for them names which come from the correlatives as in the examples already given, e.g., 'winged' from 'wing' and 'ruddered' from 'rudder'. If so, then every relative, if appropriately rendered *as such*, will be stated with reference to its reciprocal correlative, for if it were referred to a chance thing which is not its correlative, there would be no reciprocal reference. I mean that there will be no reciprocal reference even if the thing to which the relative is referred is agreed upon as having a reciprocal reference and as having the corresponding name but the relative is referred to that thing not through the name of its correlative but through the name of some other attribute of the thing. For example, if a slave is stated to be not of a master

30 but of a man or two-footed or anything of this sort, there will be no
reciprocal reference; for that to which the slave is referred is not
appropriately stated. Further, if a relative is appropriately referred to a
thing, and if the thing retains the element to which the reference is
appropriately made, the reference will always be true even if that thing
35 were to be denied of all its other attributes. Thus if a slave were referred to
a master, and if the master were to be denied of all its other attributes, such
as being two-footed and receptive of science and a man, that reference will
always be true if only the master continues being a master,[11] for it is of a
7b master that a slave is said to be the slave. But if the reference to its
correlative is not appropriately rendered, and if only that to which the
reference is made is retained but all other things belonging to it are denied,
the reference will no longer be true. For let a slave be said to be of a man
5 and a wing to be of a bird, and let the attribute of being a master be denied
of the man. Then the slave will no longer be [truly] referred to that man, for
if there is no master, neither will there be a slave. Similarly, let the attribute
of being winged be denied of a bird; then a wing will no longer be a relative,
for if the winged does not exist, neither will there be a wing of anything
10 winged. Accordingly, if a relative is referred to something, the reference
should be appropriately rendered. And if a name for the correlative exists,
the reference can be rendered easily, but if no such name exists, perhaps a
name for the correlative should be introduced. And if this is done, then it
is evident that all relatives will be reciprocally referred to correlatives.

15 Correlatives are thought to exist simultaneously by their nature, and in
most cases this is true. For when a double exists, so does the corresponding
half, and when a half exists, so does the corresponding double; and when a
master exists, so does his slave, and when a slave exists, so does his master,
and similarly with others. Moreover, they negate each other simultaneously;
20 for if no double exists, neither does a half, and if no half exists, neither does
a double; and similarly with all others of this sort.

But it is thought that not all correlatives exist simultaneously by their
nature; for the *knowable* might be thought to exist before *knowledge*. Now
25 in most cases things existed before we acquired the *knowledge* of them, for
in few cases or in no cases at all one might observe both the *knowable* and
the corresponding *knowledge* coming into existence at the same time.[12]
Further, when the *knowable* is negated, the corresponding *knowledge*, too,
is negated,[13] but when that *knowledge* is negated, the *knowable* is not
[necessarily] negated; for if the *knowable* does not exist, neither does the
30 corresponding *knowledge* (for it would not be the *knowledge* of anything),
but if that *knowledge* does not exist, nothing prevents the *knowable* from
existing. For example, in the case of the squaring of the circle, if indeed this
happens to be *knowable*, though there is no *knowledge* of it yet, it is

nevertheless *knowable*.[14] Moreover, if animals are negated, there will be no
knowledge, yet many *knowable* things may still exist.[15]

The situation with sensation is similar, for the sensible object is thought
to exist before the sensation of it exists. For when the sensible object is
negated, the sensation of it is negated also, but the sensible object is not
[necessarily] negated when the corresponding sensation is negated. For
sensations are of bodies and exist in bodies [of animals], and when the
sensibles are negated, the bodies too are negated (for what is sensible is a
body), and when bodies do not exist, neither do sensations; hence if the
sensibles are negated, sensations are negated also. But the negation of
sensations does not necessitate the negation of the sensibles; for when
animals are negated, so are sensations, but sensibles, such as bodies and
things which are hot or sweet or bitter and all the other sensibles, [may] still
exist. Again, sensations come into being at the same time as the subject
which can sense, for they come into being when animals are born, but there
are sensible objects which exist even before the sensations of them or
animals exist; for fire and water and other such, from which also animals are
composed, exist even before animals at all or their sensations exist. Hence
it would seem that sensibles may exist before the sensations of them do.[16]

There is the problem whether no substance is said to be a relative, as
indeed is thought to be the case, or whether some secondary substances may
be said to be relatives. In the case of primary substances it is true that none
of them are said to be relatives, since neither they as wholes nor their parts
are said to be relatives. For an individual man is not said to be an individual
man of some individual, nor an individual ox to be an individual ox of some
individual.[17] The same applies to the parts also; for an individual hand is not
said to be an individual hand of [or relative to] someone, though it is said to
be *the* hand of someone, and an individual head is not said to be an
individual head of [or relative to] some individual, though it is said to be *the*
head of some individual. The same applies to secondary substances, at least
to most of them. For example, a man is not said to be a man of [or relative
to] someone,[18] and an ox is not said to be an ox of some individual; and a stick
is said to be not a stick of an individual but *the property* of someone.
Evidently, then, things such as these are not relatives; but there is
disagreement concerning some secondary substances. For example, a head
is said to be the head of some animal, and a hand is said to be the hand of
someone, and similarly with others of this sort, so these might be thought to
be relatives.

Now if the definition of a relative[19] has been adequately stated, it is very
difficult or even impossible to show that no substance is said to be a relative.
If, however, it has not been adequately stated, and if a relative is that whose
being[20] is the same as being referred to some other thing in some manner,
perhaps something might be said for it. The former definition applies to all

35

8a

5

10

15

20

25

30

35   relatives, but being[21] a relative for each of them is not the same as being said, *as such*, of something else. From these remarks it is clear that, if one definitely understands something as being a relative, he will definitely understand also that to which it is said to be referred.

8b   This is evident also from the things themselves. For if one understands *this* individual as being a relative, and if to be a relative is the same as to be referred to some other thing in a certain manner, then he understands also that to which this individual is referred in that manner; for if he does not understand wholly[22] that to which this individual is referred in that manner, neither will he understand that it is referred to anything in that manner. That such is the case becomes clear if we consider individual cases.

5   For example, if one understands in a definite way that *this* individual is a double, he will immediately understand in a définite way also that of which it is the double; for if he does not understand that individual as being the double of any definite thing, neither will he understand wholly[22] that it is a double. Similarly, if a man understands *this* individual as being more beautiful, then for the same *reasons* it is necessary for him to understand immediately and in a definite way that than which that individual is more

10   beautiful. He will not just understand in an indefinite way that this individual is more beautiful than something inferior to it, since this will be an assumption and not *knowledge*; for he would not then understand with accuracy that the individual is more beautiful than something inferior to it, since it might so happen that nothing inferior to it existed. Evidently, then, it is necessary that, if a man is to understand a relative in a definite way, he

15   will have to understand in a definite way also that to which that relative is said to be related.[23]

Now in the case of a head and a hand and other such things, which are substances, a man can understand in a definite way what each of them is *as such*, but it is not necessary for him to understand that to which it is referred.[24] For one may not understand definitely whose head this head is

20   or whose hand this hand is. So these would not be relatives; and if they are not relatives, it would be true to say that no substance is a relative.

Perhaps it is difficult to speak firmly about matters such as these without having examined many cases, but to have gone through the difficulties in each case would not be without some use.

8

25   I call 'quality'[1] that in virtue of which some things[2] are said to be such and such.[3] But the name 'quality' is used in many ways.

Qualities of one kind may be called 'habits' and 'dispositions'. Habits differ from dispositions by being much more lasting and more firmly

30　established, and such are the sciences and the virtues.[4] For a science, even if moderately acquired, is thought to be firmly established with us and difficult to displace, unless a great change occurs through disease or some other such thing. The same may be said of a virtue, e.g., justice or temperance or any of this sort, for none of these is thought to be easily
35　displaced or easily changed. We call 'dispositions' those qualities, on the other hand, which are easily displaced or change quickly, e.g., a hot condition, a chill,[5] sickness, health, and things of this sort; for a man is disposed in some manner with respect to these qualities but changes
9a　quickly, becoming cold after being warm, sick after being healthy, and similarly with the others, unless any of these qualities happens to become after a long time so deep-rooted as to be incurable or very difficult to displace, in which case perhaps it should then be called a 'habit'.

5　　It is evident, then, that men intend to call 'habits' those qualities which last a very long time and are very difficult to displace, for those who have no firm possession of a science but are easily changeable are not said to have the habit of that science, though they are disposed in some way with respect to it, whether better or worse. Thus a habit and a disposition differ in this,
10　that the latter is easily displaced while the former lasts much longer and is more difficult to displace. But habits are also dispositions, whereas dispositions are not necessarily habits;[6] for those who have habits are also disposed in some way according to them, whereas those who are disposed do not in every case have a habit [corresponding to their disposition].

　　Another genus of quality is that according to which we call men, for
15　example, 'natural boxers' or 'natural runners' or 'healthy' or 'sickly', and, without qualification, those qualities which are named in virtue of some natural capability or incapability;[7] for these men are said to be such and such not just by being disposed in some manner but by having a natural capability or incapability of doing something easily or of not being affected easily. For example, men are called 'natural boxers' or 'natural runners' not
20　by being disposed in some way but by having a natural capability to do something easily; and they are called 'healthy' when they have a natural capability to resist easily being adversely affected by ordinary agents, but they are called 'sickly' when they have a natural incapability to resist easily
25　being adversely affected by ordinary agents. The same applies to hardness and softness; for a thing is called 'hard' by having the capability of not being easily divided, and it is called 'soft' by being incapable of not being easily divided.[8]

　　A third genus of qualities is that of affective qualities and affections. Such
30　are sweetness, bitterness, sourness, and all others which are akin to these; and we may add also heat, cold, whiteness, and blackness. Evidently, all these are qualities, for the things which possess them are said to be such and such with respect to them. For example, honey is called 'sweet' by virtue of

possessing sweetness, and a body is called 'white' by virtue of possessing
whiteness; and similarly with the others. Now these qualities are called
'affective' not in the sense that the objects which possess them have been
affected in some way; for it is not by having been affected in some way that
honey is called 'sweet', and likewise with other such objects. Similarly, heat
and cold are called 'affective qualities' not in the sense that the objects which
possess them have been affected in any way, but in the sense that each of
those qualities can produce on others a corresponding affection with respect
to sensation; for sweetness can produce an affection with respect to taste,
heat can produce an affection with respect to touch, and similarly with the
others.

Paleness and tan and other complexions, on the other hand, are called
'affective qualities' not in the same manner but by being the results of an
affection.[9] Clearly, many changes of color occur because of an affection; for
when a man becomes ashamed, he blushes, when he becomes afraid, he
turns pale, and so on. So even if a man has acquired by nature such an
affection arising from some physical coincidence of elements, he is likely to
have a similar complexion; for the bodily disposition of a momentary
constitution of elements arising when one is ashamed would be the same as
that of a natural constitution, so the complexion, too, would by nature be
similar in the two cases. Accordingly, all coincidences originating from
certain affections which are difficult to displace and firmly established are
called 'affective qualities'. For pallor and tan are called '[affective] qualities'
(since we are said to be such and such in virtue of them), whether they (a)
come to be in one's constitution according to nature or (b) come to be
because of a long illness or scorching and do not easily revert to their original
condition, or even stay with us throughout life; for it is in a similar way that
we are said to be such and such in virtue of them. Those which arise from
[causes] which disappear easily and which soon revert to the original
conditions, on the other hand, are called 'affections' and not 'qualities',[10] for
we are not said to be such and such in virtue of them. For neither is the man
who blushes because of shame called 'a blusher', nor is the man who turns
pale because of fear called 'a pale man', but each of them is rather said to
have been affected[11] in some way. Such things, then, are called 'affections'
and not 'qualities'.[10]

There are some qualities of the soul, too, which are similar to these, and
some of them are called 'affective qualities' while others are called
'affections'. For [conditions] which exist right from birth as a result of
certain affections, e.g., insanity and irascibility and the like, are called
'qualities', since we are said to be such and such in virtue of them, e.g., we
are called 'insane' and 'irascible', respectively. Similarly, disorders which
are not natural, but which arise from some other coincidences and are
difficult to get rid of or altogether impossible to remove, are called

5 'qualities',[10] for we are said to be such and such in virtue of them. But we call 'affections' those arising [from coincidences] which quickly revert to the original state. For example, if a man in pain is more irritable [than usual], he is not called 'irascible' by being so irritable when so affected but rather 10 'affected'. So such things are called 'affections' and not 'qualities'.[10]

A fourth genus of qualities is the shape or the *form* of each thing, and we may add to these straightness and curvature and others like them. For a thing, in virtue of each of these, is said to be such and such. For a triangle 15 or a square is said to be such and such, and so does a thing which is straight or curved.[12] And each thing, with repect to its *form*, is said to be such and such.

As for the names 'rare' and 'dense' and 'rough' and 'smooth', one would think that they signify qualities, but they seem to come under a classification which is remote from that of the genus 'quality'; for each of them appears 20 to indicate rather a certain position of the parts. A thing is called 'dense' by having its parts close to each other, but 'rare' by having its parts apart from each other; and it is called 'smooth' in view of the fact that its parts on the surface lie in some way evenly along a straight line, but 'rough' in view of the fact that some of those parts are above such a line while others are below it.[13]

25 Perhaps there are other ways in which qualities might manifest themselves, but those in the most accepted sense of the word are practically the ones we have given.

Qualities, then, are those we have mentioned, and things are called 'such and such' [or 'qualitative'] if they are derivatively named according to quality or are named in some other way from qualities. In most cases or in 30 practically all cases things are derivatively so named; for example, from 'whiteness' a thing is called 'white', from 'grammar' it is called 'grammatical', from 'justice' it is called 'just', and similarly with others. In some cases, however, a thing cannot be derivatively named from a quality because no name exists for that quality. For example, the man who is called 35 'a natural runner' or 'a natural boxer' in virtue of his natural capability is 10b not derivatively so named from any quality; for no name exists for the corresponding capability in virtue of which he is called by that name. And this is unlike the corresponding sciences according to which, as dispositions, men are called 'boxers' or 'wrestlers'; for these two sciences are called 5 'boxing' and 'wrestling', and those who are disposed according to them are derivatively called 'such and such' from them, i.e., 'boxers' and 'wrestlers', respectively.[14] In some cases a name exists for the quality, but that which is called according to that quality is not derivatively so called. For example, from integrity a man is upright,[15] for a man is called 'upright' by having integrity; but 'upright' is not derived from 'integrity'. Such situations, however, do not arise often.

10   Those things are called 'such and such', then, which are derivatively
called from the qualities mentioned or which are called from those qualities
in some other way.
        Contrariety with respect to quality is possible; for example, justice is
contrary to injustice, whiteness is contrary to blackness, and similarly with
others. And things which are named with respect to[16] a quality may be
15   contrary; for example, the unjust is contrary to the just, and the white is
contrary to the black. But this is not the case with all qualities; for there is
no contrary to red or yellow or other such colors, which are qualities.
        Again, if one of two contraries is a quality, so is the other; and this
20   becomes clear by going over the other categories. For example, justice is
contrary to injustice, and justice is a quality; and so is injustice. Injustice
cannot come under any of the other categories, for it is neither a quantity
nor a relation nor somewhere nor any of the others at all, but only a quality;
and the same applies to other contraries which are named with respect to[16]
a quality.
25   Things named by[17] a quality admit of variation of degree. One white
thing may be more white or less white than another white thing, and one
just thing may be more just than another. Moreover, a thing with a quality
may admit of that quality to a higher degree, for a white thing may become
30   more white later.[18] But it is to most things of this sort that this applies, and
not to all. For one might raise the problem whether justice admits of
variation of degree; and similarly with the other dispositions. Some thinkers
disagree about such things, for they say that we should not speak of one
instance of justice as being in any way more justice or less justice than
35   another instance, and likewise with health, but that one thing may have
11a   more health than another or have more justice than another or have more
grammatical *knowledge* than another, and similarly with the other
dispositions. Anyway, men do not dispute the fact that at least the things
which are named with respect to[16] a quality admit of variation of degree;
5   for one man may be said to be more of a grammarian or more healthy or
more just than another, and similarly with other cases. But a triangle or a
square is not thought to admit of variation of degree, nor is any other shape;
for things which admit the definition of a triangle or of a circle are all alike
triangles or circles, respectively, but things which do not admit that
10   definition cannot be [truly] said to differ in degree [as triangles or circles].
A square is no more of a circle than an oblong is, for neither of the two
admits the definition of the circle; and without qualification, if two objects
do not admit the definition of a thing proposed, neither of them can be said
to be more of that thing or less of that thing than the other. Accordingly, not
all things named by a quality admit of variation of degree.
15   Now none of the attributes we have mentioned are properties of qualities,
but things may be said to be like (or similar) or to be unlike each other only

with respect to quality; for one thing may be like another with respect to quality and nothing else. Thus it is a property of a quality that things are said to be like or unlike each other with respect to quality.[19]

20   One need not be confused by someone's remark that in our discussion of qualities we have included also many relatives; for we did say that habits and dispositions are relatives. Now in almost all such cases the genus is said to be a relative, but no particular under it is said to be a relative. For, as a
25 genus, *knowledge as such* is said to be of something else (for it is said to be the *knowledge* of something), but no particular *knowledge, as such*, is said to be of something else. For example, grammar is not said to be the grammar of something, nor music to be the music of something; but, if at all, it is with respect to their genus[20] that they are said to be relatives. Thus
30 grammar is said to be the *knowledge* of something and not the grammar of something, and music is said to be the *knowledge* of something and not the music of something. So each of these [*as such*] is not a relative. In fact, we are said to be such and such with respect to each of these since it is these that we possess; for it is by possessing a particular science that a man is said to
35 be a scientist. So it is these particular sciences that would be qualities, and it is with respect to these that we are sometimes said to be such and such, and these are not relatives.[21] Further, if the same thing should happen to be both a relative and a quality, there would be nothing absurd in listing it under both genera.[22]

9

11b   Acting and being acted upon, too, admit of contraries and of variation of degree. Thus heating is contrary to cooling, being heated is contrary to being cooled, and being pleased is contrary to being pained; so they admit
5 of contraries. And they admit of variation of degree, too; for it is possible to heat something more, or to heat it less, and also for something to be heated more, or to be heated less. So acting and being acted upon admit of variation of degree.

    So much, then, may be said concerning these [categories]. We also spoke concerning being in a position in our account of relatives, saying that it is
10 derivatively named from the corresponding position. As for the rest, i.e., at some time, somewhere, and possessing, we need not say more than what we said at the start because they are obvious; thus 'possessing' signifies such things as being shod and being armed, 'somewhere' signifies such a thing as *in the Lyceum*, and so on, as already stated.[1]

10

15   The genera we put forward have been sufficiently discussed. Concerning opposites, we should state the number of ways in which things are usually

said to be opposed.[1] Things may be opposed in four ways: (a) as a relative to its correlative, (b) as two contraries to each other, (c) as a privation to the corresponding possession, and (d) as an affirmation to the corresponding denial. Typical examples are: the double is opposed to its half as a relative to its correlative, the bad is opposed to the good as one of two contraries to the other,[2] blindness is opposed to vision as a privation to the corresponding possession, 'he sits' is opposed to 'he does not sit' as an affirmation to its denial.

Things opposed as correlatives are said, *as such*, of each other or are referred to each other in some way or other. For example, a double is said, *as such*, to be the double of another thing, for it is the double of something. Also, *knowledge* is opposed to the *known* as a relative to its correlative, and it is said, *as such*, of the *known*; and the *known* is referred, *as such*, to its opposite, which is *knowledge*, for it is said to be *known* by something, i.e., by *knowledge*. Thus things which are opposed as correlatives are said, *as such*, of each other or are referred, *as such*, to each other in some way or other.

In the case of opposites which are contraries, though they are said to be contrary to each other, they are in no way said, *as such*, to be referred to each other; for the good is said to be not the good of the bad but the contrary of the bad, and the white is said to be not the white of the black but the contrary of the black. These two kinds of opposition [i.e., correlatives and contraries], then, differ from each other.[3]

If contraries are such that either one or the other of necessity belongs[4] to the subject in which it comes to be by its nature or of which it is predicable, then they have no intermediate; but if there is no necessity for one or the other of them to belong to the subject, then they always have an intermediate. For example, disease and health by their nature come to be in the body of an animal, and it is necessary for one of them, either disease or health, to belong to the body of an animal; and 'odd' and 'even' are predicable of numbers, and it is necessary for one of them, either oddness or evenness, to belong to a given number. And between these there can be no intermediate, neither between disease and health, nor between oddness and evenness.

But if there is no necessity for any of two contraries to belong to a subject, then there is some intermediate between them. For example, blackness and whiteness by their nature come to be in a body, and it is not necessary for either of them to belong to a body; for not every body is either black or white. Again, the names 'vicious' and 'virtuous' are predicable of men and of many other subjects,[5] but it is not necessary for either one or the other to belong to the subject of which it might be predicable; for not everyone of those subjects is either vicious or virtuous. And indeed there is an intermediate between these contraries, grey or yellow or some other color between white and black, and between the vicious and the virtuous there is something which is neither vicious nor virtuous.[6] Now in some cases there are names for the intermediates, e.g., 'grey' or 'yellow' or the name of some other color between black and white; in other cases, however, there is no name available, but the intermediate is defined by the negation of both contraries, e.g., the expression 'neither good nor bad' is used for that which is between good and bad, and 'neither just nor unjust' for that which is between the just and the unjust.

A possession and its corresponding privation are concerned with the same [subject], e.g., vision and blindness are concerned with the eye. Universally speaking, that in which a possession by its nature comes to be is that with which each of the two is said to be concerned. A subject is said to be deprived of a possession which it is capable of having when that possession does not belong at all to that subject at the time at which by its nature it should belong to that subject. Thus we call 'toothless' not any subject which has no teeth, and 'blind' not any subject which has no vision, but a subject which does not have teeth or vision at the time at which by its nature it should have teeth or vision, respectively; for there are some kinds of animals which from birth have no teeth or no vision, but they are not said to be toothless or blind, respectively.

To be deprived or to have a possession is not a privation or a possession, respectively. For vision is a possession, and blindness is a privation, but to have vision is not vision, and to be blind is not blindness; for blindness is a certain privation, but to be blind is to be deprived of a certain thing and is not a privation. Further, if blindness were the same as to be blind, both would be predicable of the same subject; but though we say that a certain man is blind, we never say that he is blindness. But to be deprived and to have the corresponding possession, too, are thought to be opposed just as a privation and the corresponding possession are, since the manner of the opposition is the same; for just as blindness is opposed to vision, so being blind is opposed to having vision.[7]

The object signified by an affirmation or a denial is not itself the affirmation or the denial, respectively. For an affirmation is an affirmative statement and a denial is a negative statement, but the objects which are signified by them are not themselves statements. Yet these objects, too, are said to be opposed to each other as the corresponding affirmation and denial, since the manner of their opposition is the same; for just as an affirmation is opposed to its denial, as in the statements 'the man sits' and 'the man does not sit', so the corresponding facts under them are opposed, i.e., the man when sitting and that man when not sitting.[8]

It is evident, then, that a privation and the corresponding possession are not opposed as correlatives, since neither, *as such*, is said to be of its opposite; for vision is not the vision of blindness, nor is it said to be referred to

20   blindness in any other way. Similarly, we would not say that blindness is of
         vision; what we say is that blindness is *the privation* of vision, not *the*
         blindness of vision.[9] Moreover, in all cases correlatives are reciprocally
         referred to each other; so if blindness, *as such*, were a relative, its
         correlative, too, would be reciprocally referred to it. But there is no
25   reciprocal reference, for vision is not said to be the vision of blindness.
              That things which are said to be opposed as a possession and the
         corresponding privation, too, are not opposed as contraries is clear from
         what follows. In the case of contraries between which no intermediate exists,
         it is always necessary for one of them to belong to the subject in which it
30   comes to be by its nature or of which it is predicable; for, as already stated,
         it is between contraries one of which must belong to a subject which can
         receive it that no intermediate exists, as in the case of disease and health or
         of oddness and evenness. But in the case of contraries which have an
         intermediate, there is never a necessity for one of them to belong to every
         subject; for it is not necessary for every subject which is receptive of
         whiteness or of blackness to be either white or black, or for every subject
35   which is receptive of heat or cold to be either hot or cold, since nothing
         prevents an intermediate from belonging to that subject. Moreover, we have
         already stated that intermediates exist also between contraries neither of
         which belongs of necessity to a subject which is receptive of them, unless one
         of the contraries belongs to a subject by that subject's nature, as hotness
         belongs to fire and whiteness to snow, and to such a subject one of them must
40   definitely belong; but not either of the two; for fire cannot be cold, and snow
13a   cannot be black. So there is no necessity for one of two such contraries to
         belong to every subject which is receptive of them, but only to a subject
         which by its nature has one of them, not either of them, but a definite
         one.
              In the case of a possession and the corresponding privation, neither of the
5   above is true. First, it is not always necessary for one of them to belong to
         the subject which is receptive of them, for that which has not yet reached
         the natural state of having vision is not said to be blind or to have vision; so
         possessions and privations are not among such contraries between which
         there is no intermediate. Second, neither are they among those contraries
         between which there is an intermediate; for either the possession or the
         corresponding privation must belong to every subject which is receptive of
         them at a certain stage of the subject's existence; for when a man is at the
10   stage when he can by his nature have vision, then he will be said either to
         have vision or to be blind, not definitely to have vision, nor definitely to be
         blind, but either one of the two, since it is neither necessary that he should
         have vision nor necessary that he should be blind, but it is necessary that he
         should have just one, though either one of them. Again, in the case of
         contraries between which there is an intermediate, it was stated that there

is never a necessity for one or the other contrary to belong to the subject [which is receptive of them], except in certain subjects, and to these a definite contrary belongs. It is clear, then, that a possession and the corresponding privation are not opposed in any of the ways in which contraries are opposed.

Moreover, in the case of contraries, unless one of them belongs to a subject by the subject's nature, as hotness belongs to fire, a change in the subject from one contrary to the other is possible while the subject exists; for it is possible for that which is healthy to become sick, for that which is light to become dark, for that which is cold to become hot, for the virtuous to become vicious, and for the vicious to become virtuous. A vicious man, if directed to a better way of life and to better arguments, might make some improvement, even a little one; and, once he does this, it is evident that he might change completely or improve a great deal, for, after an initial improvement, however small, he changes more easily to virtue and is likely to improve even more. And if he keeps on doing so, he will change completely to the contrary habit, unless impeded by time. But in the case of a possession and the corresponding privation, a change in both directions is impossible; for though a change from a possession to the corresponding privation is possible, a change from a privation to the corresponding possession is impossible. No man who became blind regained his vision, no man who became bald regained his hair, and no man who lost his teeth grew a new set.

Expressions which are opposed as an affirmation to the corresponding denial are evidently not opposed in any of the ways discussed; for only in this case is it always necessary for one of the opposites to be true and the other false.[10] For neither in the case of contraries is it necessary for one of them to be true and the other false, nor in the case of correlatives or of a possession and the corresponding privation. For example, health and disease are contraries, but neither of them is true or false. Similarly, the double and the half are opposed as correlatives, but neither of the two is true or false. Things which are opposed with respect to privation and possession, too, are not true or false, as in the case of vision and blindness. In general, objects which are in no way composite expressions cannot be true or false, and the opposites[11] which we have given here as examples are not composite expressions.

One would think that contraries which are stated as composites are most likely to be true or false; for 'Socrates is healthy' is contrary to 'Socrates is sick'.[12] But not even of these composites is it always necessary for one to be true and the other false. For if Socrates exists, one of them will be true and the other false, but if Socrates does not exist, both will be false; for neither 'Socrates is sick' nor 'Socrates is healthy' is true if Socrates does not exist at all. In the case of a privation and the corresponding possession, if the subject [which might be receptive of them] does not exist at all, neither statement will be true, and if it exists, it will not always be the case that one statement is true and the other false; for 'Socrates has vision' is opposed to 'Socrates is blind'[13] as a possession to the corresponding privation, and if Socrates exists, it is not necessary for just one of them to be true or to be false (for when Socrates has not yet reached the natural state of having vision, both will be false),[14] but if Socrates does not exist at all, even then both 'Socrates has vision' and 'Socrates is blind' will be false.

In the case of an affirmation and the corresponding denial, on the other hand, it is always the case that one of them will be true and the other false, whether the subject exists or not. For if Socrates exists, it is evident that just one of the statements 'Socrates is sick' and 'Socrates is not sick' will be true or will be false, and similarly if he does not exist. For if he does not exist, 'Socrates is sick' will be false but 'Socrates is not sick' will be true.[15] Thus only expressions which are opposed as an affirmation to its denial have the property that always one will be true and the other false.

11

The contrary of a good is of necessity an evil, and this is clear by induction. For example, the contrary of health is disease, and the contrary of bravery is cowardice, and similarly with the others. The contrary of an evil, on the other hand, is in some cases a good but in others an evil. For the contrary of deficiency, which is an evil, is excess, and this is an evil; but the contrary of deficiency or of excess is also moderation, and this is a good. But such double contrariety is observed to exist in a few cases only; in most cases, the contrary of an evil is always a good.[1]

Further, in the case of contraries, if one of them exists, it is not necessary for the other to exist also. For if all animals are healthy, health will exist but not disease; and similarly, if all things are white, whiteness will exist but not blackness. Again, if Socrates in health is contrary to Socrates in disease, since both contraries[2] cannot belong to the same subject at the same time, if one of those contraries[3] exists, the other could not exist; for if Socrates in health exists, Socrates in disease cannot exist.

It is clear, too, that contraries come to be by their nature in [subjects] which are the same in species or in genus. For disease and health by their nature come to be in bodies of animals, whiteness and blackness in bodies without any qualification, and justice and injustice in the soul of a man.

It is necessary for any two contraries to be in the same genus, or to be in contrary genera,[4] or to be themselves genera. For whiteness and blackness are in the same genus (for their genus is color), justice and injustice are in contrary genera (for the genus of justice is virtue, that of injustice is vice), and good and evil are not in any genus but happen to be themselves genera[5] of other things.

12

One thing is said to be prior to another in four ways. (a) In the most fundamental way, A is said to be prior to B with respect to time, that is, if A is older than or came before B; for it is in view of a longer time that A is older than or came before B.

(b) In another way, A is said to be prior to B if A's existence follows from B's existence, but B's existence does not follow from A's existence. For example, one is prior to two; for if two exists, it follows at once that one exists,[1] but if one exists, it is not necessary for two to exist, and so the existence of two does not follow in turn from the existence of one. Thus, A is thought to be prior in existence to B if A's existence follows from B's, but B's existence does not follow from A's.

(c) In a third way, one thing is said to be prior to another according to some order, as in the case of the sciences and speeches. For in sciences which use demonstration there is an order in which one thing comes before another (for in geometry the elements come before the demonstrations,[2] and in grammar the letters of the alphabet come before the syllables); and in speeches likewise, for the introduction comes before the narrative.

There is a fourth sense of 'prior' besides those mentioned. That which is better or more honorable is thought to be prior by its nature. Ordinary men, too, usually speak of those whom they honor more or love more as having priority over those whom they honor less or love less. Perhaps this sense of the word 'prior' is far removed from the other senses.

The various senses of 'prior', then, are perhaps those given. It would seem, however, that besides these there is still another. For, of two things whose existence follows from each other, it would be reasonable to say that the one which is in any way the cause of the other is prior by nature to it. That there are such things is clear from the following. A man's existence and the truth of the statement that he exists follow from each other; for if a man exists, the statement 'a man exists' is true, and conversely, if that statement is true, a man exists. But the true statement is in no way the cause of the fact that a man exists, whereas that fact appears to be in some way the cause of the true statement; for it is by virtue of the existence or nonexistence of that fact that the statement is true or false, respectively.[3]

There are five ways, then, in which one thing is said to be prior to another.[4]

13

Things are called 'simultaneous' in an unqualified way and in the most fundamental sense if they come into being at the same time,[1] for none of

them comes into being before or after any of the rest; and such things are said to be simultaneous with respect to time. Two things are called 'simultaneous by nature' if the existence of each follows from that of the other, and if neither is the cause of the existence of the other. In the case of the double and the half, for example, the existence of each of them follows
30   from that of the other (for if the double exists, so does the half, and if the half exists, so does the double), and neither is the cause of the existence of the other.

Immediate divisions under the same genus, too, are called 'simultaneous by nature' [i.e., coordinate], and by 'immediate divisions' I mean [the
35   species] which result by the same division. For example, the feathered [species] is simultaneous by nature with the terrestrial and the aquatic[2] [species], since all these are immediate divisions under the same genus; for the genus animal is immediately divided into the feathered, the terrestrial, and the aquatic [species], and no one of these divisions is prior or posterior
15a   [by nature] to another but all three of them are thought to be simultaneous by nature.[3] Each of these [species] (terrestrial, feathered, aquatic), too, may be further divided into [lower] species, and the species resulting by the same division in each case will be simultaneous by nature. But a genus is always
5   prior [by nature] to each of its species, for the existence of the species does not follow in turn from that of the genus. For example, if an aquatic animal exists, an animal exists, but if an animal exists, it is not necessary for an aquatic animal to exist.

Things are said to be simultaneous by nature, then, (a) if the existence of
10   each follows from that of the other and is in no way the cause of the existence of the other, and (b) if they are immediate divisions under the same genus; and things are said to be simultaneous without qualification if they come into being at the same time.[4]

14

There are six kinds of motion: generation, destruction, increase, diminution, alteration, and change with respect to place [i.e., locomotion].[1]
15   It is evident that all the motions, except alteration, are distinct from each other; for a generation is not a destruction, an increase or a change with respect to place is not a diminution, and so on. But in the case of alteration there is the problem of whether the altering thing must alter[2] with respect
20   to some one of the other motions. But this is not true. For perhaps we happen to alter with respect to all or most of the affections without partaking of any of the other motions; for it is not necessary for that which is moved with respect to an affection to be increased or be diminished or be moved in any

25 other way, and so alteration would be a motion distinct from the others. For if alteration were the same as one of the other motions, then at the same time the thing in alteration would have to be increased, or be diminished, or undergo some one of the other motions; but this does not necessarily happen.[3] Similarly, that which is increased or undergoes some one of the other motions should have altered [at the same time]. But there are some

30 things which are increased without being altered. For example, when a gnomon is attached to a square in the Figure shown, the square has increased but has not altered at all,[4] and similarly with others of this kind. Hence the six motions would be distinct from each other.

15b The contrary of motion without qualification is rest[5]; but the different kinds of motion have their own contraries. Destruction is contrary to generation, diminution is contrary to increase, and rest with respect to place is contrary to change with respect to place. But a change with respect to

5 place seems to be opposed to the change towards the contrary place most of all, e.g., the motion upwards is opposed to the motion downwards, and vice versa. But of the motion that remains [i.e., of alteration], it is not easy to state what its contrary motion is. It seems that there is no contrary to it, unless one were to oppose it to rest with respect to quality or to change in the direction

10 of the contrary quality, as in the case of change with respect to place to which is opposed rest with respect to place or change towards the contrary place; for alteration is change with respect to quality. If so, then to motion with respect to quality will be opposed rest with respect to quality, or the

15 change in the direction of the contrary quality (e.g., becoming white will be opposed to becoming black), for the changes in the latter case are alterations in the direction of contrary qualities.[6]

15

The expression 'to have' is used in many senses. That which a thing is said to have may be (1) a certain habit or a certain disposition or some other quality, for we are said to have a certain *knowledge* or a certain virtue; or

20 (2) a quantity, as when one happens to have a certain height, for he is said to have a height of three cubits or four cubits; or (3) something he wears, such as a coat or a tunic, or something he wears on a part of the body, such as a ring on the hand; or (4) a part of the thing, e.g., a man is said to have a hand or a foot; or (5) something in a container, e.g., wheat in a vessel or

25 wine in a jar, for the jar is said to have wine, and the vessel is said to have wheat, and in all these cases that which is said to have has something as in a container; or (6) property, for one is said to have a house or a farm.

In yet another sense, (7) one is said to have a wife, and a wife to have a husband; but this seems to be the most remote sense of 'to have', for by 'having a wife' we mean nothing more than living with a wife.

Perhaps other senses of 'to have' might appear, but we have listed almost all the usual senses.[1]

ON PROPOSITIONS[1]

1

First we should posit what a noun is and what a verb is; then what each of the following is: a denial, an affirmation, a statement, and a sentence.[2]

Spoken expressions are symbols of mental impressions, and written expressions [are symbols] of spoken expressions.[3] And just as not all men have the same writing, so not all men make the same vocal sounds, but the things of which [all] these are primarily the signs are the same mental impressions for all men,[4] and the things of which these [mental impressions] are likenesses are ultimately the same.[5] These[6] have been discussed in my treatise *On the Soul*, for they belong to a different discipline.

Now just as in the soul there are thoughts which are neither true nor false, but also thoughts which must be either true or false, so it is with spoken expressions;[7] for truth and falsity are concerned with combination and separation.[8] Nouns and verbs by themselves (e.g., 'man' and 'the white'), when nothing else is added to them, seem to be thoughts in which nothing is combined or separated, for none of them is as yet true or false. A sign of this is the fact that even the name 'goat-stag', which signifies something, is not yet true or false unless the expression 'to be' or 'not to be' is added to it,[9] either without qualification or with a temporal qualification.[10]

2

A noun is a vocal sound which is significant by convention and has no reference to time, and of which no part is significant as [a] separate [part]. For in the name 'Greenfield' the part 'field'[1] does not by itself signify anything, though it would in the expression 'green field'. But composite nouns are not like simple nouns; for in simple nouns a part has no significance at all, whereas in composite nouns the part gives the appearance of having meaning but does not signify anything as [a] separate [part]. For example, in the word 'blackmail' the part 'mail' does not by itself signify a thing.[2] The qualification 'by convention' is added since no noun exists by nature but only when it comes into existence as a symbol.[3] Inarticulate sounds, too, like those of brutes, indicate something, but none of them is a name.

30   The expression 'not-man' is not a noun,[4] and no name exists by which such
       an expression is called; for it is neither a sentence nor a denial. But let it be
       called 'an indefinite noun', since it may belong [as a predicate] to what exists
16b   as well as to what does not exist.[5] Expressions such as 'of Philo' and 'to Philo',
       on the other hand, are not nouns but cases of a noun. In other respects, they
       have the same definition as nouns, but if 'exists' or 'existed' or 'will exist' is
       added to each of them, the resulting expression is neither true nor false,
       whereas if it is added to a noun, the resulting expression is always true or
       false. For example, 'of Philo exists' and 'of Philo does not exist' are in no way
5   true or false.

3

       A verb is [a name] (a) which includes in its meaning also time, (b) of which
       no part as [a] separate [part] has any meaning, and (c) which is always a sign
       of something said about something else.[1] By 'includes in its meaning also
       time' I mean, for example, that while 'recovery' is a noun, 'recovers' is a
10   verb,[2] for a verb includes in its meaning also time, e.g., present time. In
       addition, it is always a sign of something said about something else, e.g., of
       something said of a subject or present in a subject.
       Expressions such as 'is not healthy' and 'is not sick' I do not call 'verbs';
       for though they also include time in their meaning and always belong to
       something, no name has been posited to indicate their difference from
15   verbs. Such expressions will be called 'indefinite verbs', and they may
       belong to what exists as well as to what does not exist. Similarly, 'was
       healthy' and 'will be healthy' are not verbs but tenses[3] of a verb; and they
       differ from verbs in that verbs include in their meaning present time while
       tenses of a verb include time outside the present.[4]
20   Now verbs stated by themselves are names and signify something (for he
       who uses them pauses in his thought and the hearer is at ease), but they do
       not yet signify that something is or is not the case; for neither are 'to be' and
       'not to be' signs of any fact,[5] nor is 'being' a sign of a fact[5] when used by itself
       as a participle, for each of these [i.e., 'to be', 'not to be', 'being'] by itself
25   signifies nothing but a sort of combination which cannot be thought without
       the [things] which are combined.

4

       A sentence is a vocal sound significant by convention, some part of which,
       taken by itself, has meaning as an utterance[1] but not as an affirmation or a
       denial.[2] I mean, for example, that 'man' signifies something, but not that
30   something is[3] or is not the case; and it is by the addition of something else
       [to it] that an affirmation or a denial may be formed. But no syllable of
       'virtue' [has any meaning by itself], for the part 'use', too, in the word

'mouse' has no meaning [as a part] but is only a vocal sound.[4] A part of a composite word, on the other hand, may have meaning, as stated earlier,[5] but not taken by itself [as a part].

17a

Every sentence has meaning, not as a natural instrument but, as stated earlier,[6] by convention. Not all sentences are declarative, however, but only those to which truth or falsity belongs. Thus truth or falsity does not belong

5

to all sentences; for example, a prayer is a sentence but is neither true nor false. So let all sentences which are neither true nor false be dismissed here, for their consideration is more appropriate to rhetoric or to poetics. Our present inquiry is about declarative[7] sentences [i.e., propositions].

5

Of propositions, that which is primarily one is an affirmation,[1] the next is

10

a denial; and each of the rest is one by conjunction.[2] Every proposition must have a verb or a tense of a verb [as a part]; for even the definition[3] of man is not yet a proposition, until 'is' or 'was' or 'will be' or something of this sort is added to it. Of course, one may ask why the expression 'two-footed terrestrial animal' is one and not many; for it is one not by the fact that the

15

words are stated together. The discussion of this problem, however, belongs to another discipline.[4] Now a proposition is one either by indicating one [object][5] or by being one by conjuntion; but we have many propositions if many [objects] are indicated or if the [propositions] are not conjoined.[6]

Let a noun or a verb be called just 'an utterance', since one cannot use such a vocal sound as a statement to indicate something, whether as an

20

answer to a question, or not as an answer but as something he himself intends to state.

Of propositions, those which are simple are statements, i.e., [sentences] in which something is affirmed of something else or is denied of it, and the others, which are composed of statements, are like sentences which are combined. A simple statement[7] is a vocal sound signifying the existence[8] or the nonexistence of something according to one of the divisions of time.[9]

6

25

An affirmation is a statement affirming something of something else; a denial is a statement denying something of something else. Now since it is possible (a) to state of something which exists[1] that it does not exist, and of something which does not exist that it exists, and of something which exists that it exists, and of something which does not exist that it does not exist, and (b) in a similar way to state of something that it exists or does not exist at

30   a time lying outside the present, then in each of the above cases a man might
      deny what another man has affirmed or affirm what another man has
      denied. Clearly, then, to every affirmation there is an opposite[2] denial and
      to every denial there is an opposite affirmation. And let an affirmation and
      its opposite denial taken together be called 'a contradiction'.[3] By 'opposition'
35   here I mean the opposition of the same predicate with respect to the same
      subject, without using the subject or the predicate equivocally; and we
      include other such qualifications to meet sophistical captiousness.[4]

                                    7

      Since some things[1] are universal but others are [predicable of an]
40   individual (by 'universal' I mean that which by its nature is predicable of
      more than one, and by 'individual' I mean that which is not [so predicable],
17b   e.g., man [or 'man'] is a universal but Callias [or 'Callias'] is [predicable of]
      an individual), a statement of something as existing or as not existing must
      sometimes be stated of a universal and sometimes of an individual.
      If one states universally of a universal [subject] that something is and also
5   that it is not the case, the two statements will be contrary. By 'stating
      universally of a universal' I mean, for example, 'every man is white' and 'no
      man is white.'[2] On the other hand, if one states of a universal [subject], but
      not universally, [that something is and also that it is not the case], the two
      statements are not contrary, but the things indicated may sometimes be
      contrary.[3] By 'stating of a universal, but not universally' I mean, for
10   example, 'man is white' and 'man is not white' [or 'men are white' and 'men
      are not white'];[4] for though [the subject] 'man' is universal, it is not
      universally used in the statement, for the word 'every' signifies not a
      universal but something universally taken. But if a predicate which is a
      universal is universally taken, then it cannot be truly predicable [of a
15   subject]; for there can be no true affirmation in which such predicate, taken
      universally, is predicable of a subject. For example, 'every man is every
      animal' is false.
      I maintain that an affirmation is opposed to a denial in a contradictory
      way if both have the same subject and predicate but one of them [i.e., of the
      contradictories] is universally taken while the other is the denial thereof.[5]
      For example, 'every man is white' and 'not every man is white' are
20   contradictories, and so are 'no man is white' and 'some men[6] are white'. But
      if both the affirmation and the denial are universal,[7] [then I maintain that]
      the two statements are opposed in a contrary way.[8] For example, 'every man
      is white' and 'no man is white' are contraries, and so are 'every man is just'
      and 'no man is just'. Hence both members of a pair of contraries here cannot
      be true at the same time;[9] but the contradictories of a pair of contraries may

25   sometimes be true of the same subject at the same time, as in the case of 'not every man is white' and 'some men are white'.

    Of a pair of contradictory statements with a universal subject universally taken,[10] one of them must be true and the other false; and such is also the case if the subject is an individual, as in 'Socrates is white' and 'Socrates is not white'.[11] But of a pair [of contradictory statements][12] with a universal

30   subject which is not universally taken, it is not always the case that one of them is true and the other false.[13] For it is possible to state truly that men are white and also that men are not white, that men are noble and also that men are not noble; for if a man is disgraceful, he is not noble, or if he is becoming [noble], still he is not noble.[14] At first, this fact would seem absurd,

35   because 'men are not white' appears to mean also that no man is white; but neither does 'men are not white' mean what 'no man is white' does, nor is it necessary [for the two statements to be both true or both false] at the same time.

    It is also evident that corresponding to one affirmation there is just one

40   denial; for what a denial should do is to deny the same thing which the affirmation affirms, and of the same subject, whether the subject be (a) an

18a   individual or (b) a universal, and whether a universal subject is universally taken or not. For example, the denial of 'Socrates is white' is 'Socrates is not white'. But if the affirmation and the denial have different predicates or different subjects,[15] they are not opposed to each other but are different. The

5   denial of 'every man is white', then, is 'not every man is white'; the denial of 'some men are white' is 'no man is white'; and the denial of 'men are white' is 'men are not white'.

    We have stated, then, that (a) to one affirmation there is opposed in a contradictory manner just one denial and have indicated what those

10   statements are; that (b) contrary statements are different from contradictory statements and what these are; and that (c) not every pair of contradictories is such that one statement in it is true and the other false, why this is so, and when one statement in such a pair must be true and the other false.[16]

8

    A [statement] is one affirmation or one denial if it signifies [something which is] about [a subject which is] one, whether the [subject] is a universal

15   taken universally, or not.[1] Such statements are 'every man is white' and 'not every man is white', 'men are white' and 'men are not white', 'no man is white' and 'some men are white', provided that the word 'white' has one meaning. If in a statement the name posited has two meanings which cannot make up something which is one, then the statement is not one affirmation

20   or one denial. For example, if one were to posit the name 'coat' as meaning

a horse and also a man in 'coats are white', this statement would not be one affirmation, nor [would the corresponding denial be] one denial; for the affirmation would not differ from the statement 'men and horses are white', and this itself would not differ from the two statements 'horses are white' and 'men are white'. Accordingly, if these [two statements] signify many

25 [objects] and are many, it is clear that the first [statement], too, signifies many [objects], or else nothing at all (for an individual man is not a horse).[2] So in contradictory statements of this sort, too, it is not necessary for one of the statements to be true and the other false.[3]

9

In the case of that which exists or has occurred, it is necessary for the corresponding affirmation or its denial to be true, or to be false.[1] And in the

30 case of two contradictories with a universal subject universally taken, or with an individual subject, it is always necessary for one of them to be true and the other false, as we stated; but if the subject is a universal without being universally taken, there is no such necessity, and we stated this fact too.[2] Concerning future particulars,[3] on the other hand, the situation is not similar.[4]

35 First, if every affirmation and every denial is either true or false,[5] then it is necessary for every object, too, either to be or not to be. Accordingly, if one man says that something will be the case while another man denies this, then clearly it is necessary for just one of them to be speaking truly if an affirmation or a denial is either true or false, for in such cases both will not

18b exist at the same time.[6] For if it were true to say that a thing is white (or not white), it would be necessary for the thing to be white (or not white), and if it is white (or not white), then it would be true to affirm that it is (or to deny it); and if the thing is not as stated, the statement is false, and if the statement is false, the thing is not as stated. Accordingly, either the

5 affirmation or the denial must be true, or must be false.[7]

If so, [it would appear that] nothing occurs by chance or in either of two ways; nor will it so occur in the future or fail to so occur, but everything [will occur, or will fail to occur,] of necessity and not in either of two ways. For either he who affirms a future event will speak truly or he who denies it; otherwise the event would be just as likely to occur as not to occur, for that which may occur in either of two ways does not occur or will not occur in one way more than in the other.

10 Again, if a thing is white now, it was true to say earlier that it would be white; so concerning an event which has taken place, it was always true to say 'it is' or 'it will be'.[8] And if it was always true to say 'it is' or 'it will be', the event was not of such a nature as not to be or not to come to be; and if

15

it was not of such a nature as not to occur, it was impossible for it not to occur; and if was impossible for it not to occur, it was necessary for it to occur. So [it appears that] all future events will occur of necessity. Hence nothing will come to be in either of two ways or by chance,[9] for if it will occur by chance, it will not occur of necessity.

20

Further, one cannot [truly] say of an event that neither the affirmation nor the denial is true, i.e., that the event will neither occur nor fail to occur. Otherwise, if the affirmation is false, the denial [will] not [be] true, and if the denial is false, it turns out that the affirmation [will] not [be] true.[10] In addition, if it is true to say [of a thing] that it is white and large, both [these attributes] will have to belong [to the thing], and if [it is true to say that] they will belong [to the thing] tomorrow, then they will [have to] belong to it tomorrow.[11] But if an event will neither occur nor fail to occur tomorrow, there would be no happening [tomorrow] in either of two ways, e.g., a sea fight would neither have to occur nor have to fail to occur tomorrow.

25

30

These and other such absurdities would indeed result, if of every affirmation and its denial, whether with a universal subject taken universally or with an individual subject, it were necessary [12] for one of the opposites to be true and the other false, and if, of things in the process of becoming, that which would be or which would come to be could not be in either of two ways but of necessity only one of them, in which case there would be no need to deliberate or take *action* with the expectation that, if we act in a certain way, a certain result will come about, but if we do not, it will not come about. For nothing prevents one man from saying now that a certain event will occur ten thousand years hence, and another from saying that the event will not occur; and so that alternative [occurrence or non-occurrence], of which it was at one time true to state that it will come to be, would of necessity come to be [at a later time]. Further, neither would it make any difference whether some men make the contradictory statements or not, for it is clear that things would be such even if neither the affirmation nor the denial were stated; for events would, or would not, occur not because we have affirmed or denied them, and [they would occur, or not occur,] no less if we had said so ten thousand years earlier rather than any other period of time. So if at all times things were such that [a definite] one of two contradictory statements [about the future] would be true, then what that statement says would of necessity come to be, and each [future] occurrence would always be such as to come to be of necessity. For that of which someone stated truly that it will be would not be of such a nature as to fail to occur, and of [such] an occurrence it was always true to say [earlier] that it will be.

35

19a

5

Now these things are impossible; for we observe that principles[13] of things which will occur arise both from deliberations and from *actions*, and that,

10   in general, objects which do not exist always in *actuality* have alike the
     potentiality of existing and of not existing; and objects which may be or may
     not be may also come to be or may not come to be.[14] It is clear, too, that there
     are many objects which have such [a nature]. For example, this coat has the
     potentiality of being cut to pieces [at a certain time later] but may wear out
15   before being so cut. Similarly, it has the potentiality of not being so cut; for
     if it did not have this potentiality, it could not have the potentiality of
     wearing out before.[15] Such is also the case with the other kinds of
     generations which are said to possess such potentiality. It is evident, then,
     that it is not of necessity that all things exist or are in the process of coming
     to be; in some cases a thing may come to be in either of two ways, in which
20   case the affirmation of each alternative is no more true than the denial of
     it, whereas in other cases one of the two alternatives is more likely to occur
     and in most cases it does occur, but the less likely alternative may still come
     to be [*actually*].

     Now when a thing exists, it does so of necessity, and when a nonbeing does
     not exist, it is of necessity that it does not exist;[16] but it is not of necessity that
25   every existing thing exists or that every nonbeing does not exist. For it is not
     the same for a thing to exist of necessity when it exists and for that thing to
     exist of necessity without qualification, and similarly with nonbeing. The
     same remarks apply to any two contradictories also.[17] Thus everything of
     necessity either is or is not, and everything of necessity will either be or not
     be;[18] but one cannot [always truly] state that a definite one of the two
30   alternatives is or will be of necessity.[19] I mean, for example, that a sea fight
     will of necessity[20] either take place tomorrow or not; but a sea fight will not
     necessarily take place tomorrow, nor will it necessarily fail to take place
     either, though it will of necessity[20] either take place tomorrow or fail to take
     place. So since statements are true in a way which is similar to the
     corresponding facts, it is clear that if objects are such that they may turn out
35   in either of two ways or may admit contraries, the two contradictory
     statements corresponding to them are of necessity related in a similar
     manner. And such indeed is the case with objects which do not always exist
     or which are not always nonexistent. For though one of the two
     contradictories concerning these objects must be true (or false), it is not
     [definitely] the affirmation, nor [definitely] the denial, that will be true but
     either one of them; and one of them may be more likely to be true,[21] but not
     already true (or already false) at the time [when a man states it]. Clearly,
19b then, it is not necessary in the case of every affirmation and its opposite
     denial [concerning future particulars] that one of them be [definitely] true
     and the other [definitely] false; for the situation with objects which do not
     exist but have the potentiality of existing and of not existing is not like that
     of existing things,[22] but as we have stated.

10

Since an affirmation signifies something affirmed of something, and since
the [subject of an affirmation] is a noun or something without a name, and
since in the affirmation both the [predicate][1] should be one and the subject
should be one (we have already discussed the noun and that which has no
name;[2] for I said that 'not-man' is not a noun but an indefinite noun, since
it, too, signifies in some way something which is one, and in the same way
'is not healthy' is not a verb but an indefinite verb), every affirmation and
every denial will be composed of a noun and a verb, each of which may be
definite or indefinite. Thus there can be no affirmation or denial without a
[definite or indefinite] verb; for the expressions 'is', 'will be', 'was', 'is
becoming', and all other such are posited to be verbs, since they also signify
time [in addition to signifying what is said about a subject].

Accordingly, the primary affirmation and denial are, to use an example,
'man exists' and 'man does not exist', then 'not-man exists' and 'not-man
does not exist'; and again 'every man exists' and 'not every man exists', and
then 'every not-man exists' and 'not every not-man exists'. And the same
statements may be made for times other than the present.

When the word 'is' in the statement is added to the predicate as a third
element, then the oppositions can be stated in two ways. I mean by this, for
example, that in 'man is just' the word 'is' in that affirmation is a third
element, whether a name or a verb.[3] So because of this fact there arise four
statements, [and in] two of them [the predicates] are related to an affirmation
and its denial as a pair of privations [of 'just'], but [in] the other two [the
predicates are related] not [as privations].[4] By this I mean that the word 'is'
may come before either 'just' or 'not-just', and so may the negation [i.e., 'is
not']; hence four statements arise. The Diagram below will give us an idea
of what we are saying.

    (a) man is just ⟵   ⟶ (b) man is not just
    (d) man is not not-just ⟵   ⟶ (c) man is not-just[5]

Here the expression 'is' or 'is not' comes before 'just' and also before
'not-just'. Such, then, is the arrangement of these statements, as we stated in
the [Prior] Analytics.[6] A similar situation arises even if the affirmation has
as a subject a noun which is universally taken, as in the Diagram below.

    (A) every man is just ⟵   ⟶(B) not every man is just
    (D) not every man is not-just ⟵   ⟶(C) every man is not-just[7]

But here the statements joined by a diagonal line cannot be both true in the
same manner as in the previous case, though at times both may be true.[8]

These, then, are two pairs of opposites; but two other pairs arise if to
'not-man' as a subject [a verb or an indefinite verb] is added. Thus:

    not-man is just ⟵   ⟶ not-man is not just
    not-man is not not-just ⟵   ⟶ not-man is not-just

There can be no other oppositions besides these. The last two pairs form by themselves[9] a group distinct from the previous pairs since they use 'not-man' as a noun.[10]

5

10

15

Whenever the word 'is' does not fit in the statement, e.g., when the verb is 'recovers'[11] or 'walks', the effect of such verb is the same as that when the word 'is' is added: for example, 'every man recovers', 'not every man recovers', 'every not-man recovers', 'not every not-man recovers'. We should not use 'not-every man', but the negation 'not' should be added to 'man'; for the word 'every' signifies not a universal but [a subject] universally taken. This fact becomes clear from the following pairs: 'man recovers' and 'man does not recover', and 'not-man recovers' and 'not-man does not recover'; and these last two pairs differ from the first two pairs in that their subject is not universally taken. Thus the words 'every' and 'no' mean nothing else than that the noun [which is the subject] in an affirmation or a denial is universally taken, but the other parts to be added should remain the same.

20

25

30

Since the contrary of 'every animal is just' is 'no animal is just', it is evident that (a) these two statements cannot be true at the same time and of the same subject[12] but that (b) their opposites [i.e., their contradictories], that is, 'not every animal is just' and 'some animals are just', may sometimes be true [at the same time and of the same subject]. Also, 'no man is just' follows from 'every man is not-just', and the opposite of the latter, which is 'not every man is not-just', follows from 'some men are just', for there must be a just man.[13] It is also evident that if, concerning an individual, a denial is a true answer to a question, then a [related] affirmation is also true concerning that individual. For example, if 'Socrates is not wise' is a true answer to the question 'Is Socrates wise?', then 'Socrates is not-wise' is also true.[14] In universal statements, on the other hand, the corresponding affirmation is not similarly true, but the denial is true. For example, if the statement 'every man is wise' is not true, then the statement 'every man is not-wise' is false[15] but 'not every man is wise' is true; for the latter is the opposite [i.e., the contradictory], whereas the other is the contrary.[16]

35

Opposites which are indefinite nouns or indefinite verbs, like 'not-man' and 'not-just', [17] might be thought to be like denials without a noun or a verb, but they are not denials; for a denial must always be true or false, but he who says 'not-man' without adding anything else is no closer to saying something true or false than he who says 'man' but is even further away.[18]

40

The statement 'every not-man is just' does not have the same meaning as any of the above statements, nor does its opposite [i.e., its contradictory], which is 'not every not-man is just'. But the statement 'every not-man is not-just' has the same meaning as 'no not-man is just'.[19]

20b

If nouns and verbs are transposed, the meanings of the resulting statements remain the same, e.g., 'man is white' and 'white is man' have the

同

same meaning;[20] for if not, there would be many denials of the same thing. But we have shown that an affirmation has just one denial[21]. For the denial of 'man is white' is 'man is not white'; but if 'white is man' does not mean what 'man is white' does, its denial would be either 'white is not not-man' or 'white is not man'.[22] But the former of the last two statements is the denial of 'white is not-man', whereas the latter is the denial of 'man is white',[23] and so there would be two different denials of one statement. Clearly, then, if the name and the verb are transposed, the meaning of an affirmation or of a denial remains the same.

11

An expression in which one [thing] is affirmed or denied of many [things], or many [things] are affirmed or denied of one [thing], is not one affirmation or one denial unless that which is indicated by 'many [things]' is some one [thing]. By 'one [thing]' I do not mean [things] for which one name is posited but which do not make up one [thing]. For example, a man is perhaps an animal and two-footed and tame, and these three make up something which is one.[1] But whiteness[2] and man and walking do not make up [something which is] one; so if someone affirms of these something which is one or affirms these of something which is one, though he does so with one vocal sound, that sound is not one affirmation but many.[3] Accordingly, if a dialectical question [with many predicates or many subjects which do not make up one thing] is a request for an answer, whether as a premise or as one part of a contradiction (and a premise is one of the two parts in a contradiction), there can be no single answer to such a question, even if the answer were true,[4] for neither is the question single. We have discussed these matters in the *Topics*.[5] It is also clear that the question 'what is it?' is not dialectical; for, from a dialectical question, the man who answers should be given the choice of stating whichever part of a contradiction he wishes. Thus the questioner should specify, for example, whether a man is so-and-so or not.

Since some things which are predicable [of a subject] separately are predicable [of it] when combined as if the combination were one predicate,[6] whereas others cannot be so predicable when combined, what is the difference [between the two kinds of combined predicates]? For example, it is true to say of a man separately that he is an animal and that he is two-footed and also to combine the two into one [and say that he is a two-footed animal], and likewise to say of a man that he is a man and that he is white, and to combine these two into one [predicate and say that he is a white man]. But if a man is a shoemaker and also good, we cannot truly say from these that he is a good shoemaker.[7] For if we were to say, whenever each predicate is truly said of a subject separately, that the combination of the two should be a predicate of it also, many absurdities would follow. For example, it is true to say of a [white] man that he is a man and also white, and hence that he is a white man; and since he is white and also a white man, it would be true to say of him that he is a white white man, and so on to infinity. Again, if a man is musical and white and walking, these three, too, could be combined many times indefinitely. Again, since 'Socrates' and 'man' are predicable of Socrates, so would 'Socrates Socrates man'; and since 'man' and 'two-footed' are predicable of him, so would 'two-footed man man'.

Clearly, then, many absurdities would follow if one were to say without making any qualification that predicates could be combined. Let us now posit how predicates may be combined.

Of predicates and the subjects of which they happen to be predicable, those which are predicable accidentally,[8] whether of the same subject or of each other, cannot be [combined to form] one [predicate]. For example, if a man is both pale and musical, 'pale' and 'musical'[9] cannot as two words be one [predicate], for both are accidental to the same subject. Neither can the expression 'musical pale' [or 'musically pale'] be one [predicate] if it were true to say that the pale is musical; for it is by accident that the musical is pale, and so 'pale musical' cannot be one predicate. It is in view of this fact that neither can a man, who is a shoemaker and also good, be [truly] called 'a good shoemaker' in an unqualified way; but he is truly called 'a two-footed animal', for it is not by accident that he is two-footed and an animal.[10]

Again, predicates which are such that one of them is included in the other cannot combine to form one predicate. In view of this fact, neither can 'pale' be added to itself many times, nor can one call a man 'animal man' or 'two-footed man', for 'animal' and 'two-footed' are included in 'man'. On the other hand, it is true to say of an individual [what he is or happens to be] without qualification, e.g., to call an individual man 'a man', and an individual pale man 'a pale man'.[11] But such cannot always be the case, for when in one of the predicates there is something which is opposed to the other predicate and so leads to a contradiction in the combined predicate, it is not true but false to predicate each predicate of the individual, e.g., it is false to predicate 'man' of a dead man;[12] but if no such opposite exists, it is true to predicate of an individual each of the combined predicates. Or better, when an opposite element is present, it is never true to predicate of an individual each predicate separately, but when no such element is present, it is not always true to predicate each element of an individual. From the statement 'Homer is a poet', for example, does the statement 'Homer is' follow or not? But the word 'is' in the former statement is accidentally predicable of Homer, for it is not the word 'is' by itself that is

30 predicable of Homer but [the verb] 'is a poet'. Accordingly, whenever definitions are substituted for the names in a combined predicate which contains no contrariety, if the elements are essential and not accidental predicates, it would be true to predicate [of the individual] an element [of the combined predicate] even without qualification.[13] But the fact that nonbeing is an object of opinion does not make the statement 'nonbeing is' true; for the opinion of nonbeing is that it is not, not that it is.[14]

12

35 Having made these distinctions, we must next consider how denials and affirmations concerning what is possible and what is not possible [to be or not to be], and what may and what cannot [be or not be], and what is impossible and what is necessary [to be or not to be] are related to each other; for some difficulties arise.

Composite expressions with respect to the verbs 'to be' and 'not to be' are opposed to each other as contradictories in the following manner. For
21b example, the denial of 'to be a man' is 'not to be a man' but not 'to be a not-man'; and the denial of 'to be a white man' is 'not to be a white man' but not 'to be a not-white man' (for if not, since the affirmation or the denial
5 is true in every case, it would be true to say that wood is a not-white man.[1]) Since such is the case, the same will be true also of statements which do not have the verb 'to be' but some other verbal expression in its place. For example, the denial of 'man walks' is not 'not-man walks' but 'man does not
10 walk'; for it makes no difference whether one says 'man walks' or 'man is walking.'[2]

If the preceding argument were true in all other cases, then the denial of 'possible to be',[3] too, would be 'possible not to be' and not 'not possible to be'. But it is thought that the same thing is possible both to be and not to be; for everything which is capable of being cut or of walking is also capable of not being cut or of not walking, respectively. The reason for this truth is the fact
15 that everything which has such possibility does not always have the corresponding *actuality*,[4] and so the negation,[5] too, would belong to that thing; for that which is capable of walking is also capable of not walking, and that which is capable of being seen is also capable of not being seen. But it is impossible for opposite assertions to be truly asserted of the same thing[6]
[at the same time]; hence the denial of 'possible to be' is not 'possible not to
20 be'. For it follows from what has been said that either (a) the same [predicate] can be asserted and denied of the same object at the same time or (b) assertions and negations here are formed not by the additions of 'to be' and 'not to be', respectively. So if alternative (a) is impossible, alternative (b) should be chosen. Thus the denial of 'possible to be' is 'not possible to be'.

25   The same argument applies to 'may be' also, for the denial of this, too, is 'cannot be'.[7] A similar argument applies to the others, too, i.e., to the necessary and to the impossible. For, just as in the previous cases 'to be' and 'not to be' are the additions determining truth and falsity, whereas the things underlying them are [subjects such as] 'white' and 'man', so here 'to
30   be' and 'not to be' become like subjects, while 'it is possible' and 'it may' [and their opposites] become the additions which determine truth or falsity.

      The denial of 'possible not to be', then, is not 'possible to be'[8] but 'not
35   possible not to be', and the denial of 'possible to be' is not 'possible not to be' but 'not possible to be'. It is in view of this, too, that 'possible to be' and 'possible not to be' would be thought to follow each other, for one would think that the same thing is possible to be as well as possible not to be; for expressions such as 'possible to be' and 'possible not to be' are not contradictories. The expressions 'possible to be' and 'not possible to be', on
22a   the other hand, are never true of the same thing at the same time, for they are opposites; and the expressions 'possible not to be' and 'not possible not to be' are likewise never true of the same thing at the same time. Similarly, the denial of 'necessary to be' is not 'necessary not to be' but 'not necessary
5   to be', and the denial of 'necessary not to be' is 'not necessary not to be'; and the denial of 'impossible to be' is not 'impossible not to be', but 'not impossible to be', while the denial of 'impossible not to be' is 'not impossible not to be'.

      Universally, then, as we have stated, the expressions 'to be' and 'not to be' should be posited as subjects, but the others [i.e., 'possible' and 'not possible',
10   etc.] should be posited as additions to these to produce affirmations and denials; and the following should be regarded as the opposite assertions:[9]

Table I

possible	not possible
may	can not
impossible	not impossible
necessary	not necessary
true	not true[10]

13

      If these expressions are posited in this manner, the logical consequences
15   are as follows. From 'possible to be' follow (a) 'may be', and conversely,[1] and also (b) 'not impossible to be' and 'not necessary to be';[2] from 'possible not to be' and 'may not be' follow 'not necessary not to be' and 'not impossible not to be'; from 'not possible to be' and 'can not be' follow 'necessary not to be' and 'impossible to be'; and from 'not possible not to be' and 'can not not

20   be' follow 'necessary to be' and 'impossible not to be'. What has been stated may be viewed from the Table which follows.[3]

Table II

A_1: possible to be	B_1: not possible to be
A_2: may be	B_2: can not be
A_3: not impossible to be	B_3: impossible to be
A_4: not necessary to be	B_4: necessary not to be
C_1: possible not to be	D_1: not possible not to be
C_2: may not be	D_2: can not not be
C_3: not impossible not to be	D_3: impossible not to be
C_4: not necessary not to be	D_4: necessary to be

Now 'impossible' and 'not impossible' follow from 'may' and 'possible' and from 'can not' and 'not possible' in a contradictory but converse manner, for the denial of 'impossible [to be]' follows from 'possible to be' and the affirmation [i.e., 'impossible [to be]'] follows from the denial [i.e., from 'not possible to be']; for 'impossible to be' follows from 'not possible to be' since 'impossible to be' is an affirmation, whereas 'not impossible to be' is a denial.[4]

We should next consider how statements containing the word 'necessity' are related. Evidently, they are not related in the manner in which they are placed; the contraries do follow, but the contradictories are separate.[5] For the denial of 'necessary not to be' is not 'not necessary to be', since both statements may be true of the same thing [at the same time], for that which is necessary not to be is not necessary to be.[6] The *reason* that statements containing the word 'necessity' do not follow in the same way as the other statements is the fact that the word 'impossible', when added to a contrary subject, amounts to the same thing[7] as the word 'necessary'. For if P is impossible to be, then P is necessary not to be, but not necessary to be; and if P is impossible not to be, then P is necessary to be. Thus if the others [i.e., 'not impossible' and 'impossible'] follow from 'possible' and 'not possible', respectively, in a manner which is similar,[8] these follow in a contrary manner since 'necessary' and 'impossible' do not have the same meaning but, as we stated, are inversely related.

But is it not impossible to posit the contradictories of 'it is necessary' in this manner?[9] For that which is necessary to be is possible to be. For if not, the denial would follow (since one must either assert or deny something of something); but if it is not possible to be, it is impossible to be, and so that which is necessary to be would be impossible to be, a conclusion which is indeed absurd.[10] Moreover, from 'possible to be' follows 'not impossible to be', and from the latter follows 'not necessary to be'; and so it turns out that what is necessary to be is not necessary to be, a conclusion which is indeed absurd.[11] Further, neither 'necessary to be' nor 'necessary not to be' follows from 'possible to be'; for what is possible to be admits of two alternatives [i.e., it is also possible not to be], whereas if either of the other two statements were true, those two alternatives would not be true. For that which is possible to be is at the same time possible not to be, but if it were necessary to be, or necessary not to be, it would not have the possibility of both alternatives.[12] What remains, then, is that 'not necessary not to be' follows from 'possible to be'[13] (for the same is true with respect to 'necessary to be' also),[14] for this[15] becomes also the contradictory of that which follows from 'not possible to be'; for from 'not possible to be' follows 'impossible to be' and 'necessary not to be', and the denial of the latter is 'not necessary not to be'. Accordingly, these contradictories, too, follow in the manner stated, and nothing impossible happens if they are posited in this way.

One may raise the problem whether 'possible to be' follows from 'necessary to be'. For if not, then 'not possible to be' would follow, which is the contradictory [of 'possible to be']; or, if one were to say that 'not possible to be' is not the contradictory, then one must say that 'possible not to be' is the contradictory. But both of these are false of that which is necessary to be. On the other hand, the same thing is thought to have the possibility of being cut and of not being cut, of existing and of not existing, and so that which is necessary to be might not be; and this conclusion, too, is false.[16]

Now it is evident that not everything which is possible to be or to walk has also the possibility of the opposite,[17] but that there are some things of which [the possibility of the opposite is] not true. Of these, there are those which have a capability but not according to reason, like fire, which has the capability of heating but has a nonrational capability.[18] Accordingly, some capabilities exist [in persons] with reason and are capabilities leading to many[19] and also to contrary things; and, of nonrational capabilities, not all [lead to many or to contrary things], as we said. Thus fire does not have the capability of heating and also of not heating, nor do those things which exist always in *actuality*.[20] But there are also things which have at the same time the possibility of admitting opposites with respect to their nonrational capabilities.[21] But we are stating this point for the sake of pointing out that not every capability is a capability for opposites, not even those [in some cases] which are said to be capabilities of the same kind.[22] Some are called 'capabilities' equivocally. For the word 'possible' does not have a single meaning, but in one way 'to be possible' is to be true when the thing signified exists *actually*. For example, we say that a man is capable of walking when he is [*actually*] walking, and, in general, we say 'it is possible to be' when that which is said to be possible is already existing in *actuality*; but we say such things also when the object might come to be *actualized*, e.g., we say 'it is possible for him to walk', meaning that he might walk.[23] The latter capability exists only in things which can be in motion, but the former exists also in immovable things.[24] It is true to say of each of these that it is not impossible to walk (or to be), that is, of that which is now walking (or is in *actuality*) and also of that which has the capability of walking [but is not now walking]. Accordingly, although it is not true to say of that which is necessary in an unqualified way that it is capable in the latter way, it is true to say of it that it is capable in the former way.[25] So since the universal[26] follows from the particular, that which is of necessity is also possible, but not possible in every sense of the word 'possible'. And so perhaps the necessary and that which is not necessary are the principles of what is or is not, and the rest should be regarded as following from these.[27]

It is evident from what has been said that that which exists of necessity exists in *actuality*; so since eternal things are prior, *actuality* is prior to potentiality also.[28] And some things are *actualities* without potentiality, namely, the first substances,[29] others are *actualities* with potentiality, and these are prior by nature but posterior in time,[30] and then there are those which are never *actualities* but are only potentialities.[31]

14

One may raise the question whether an affirmation is contrary to the corresponding denial or to a [related] affirmation, and whether the statement 'every man is just' is contrary to 'no man is just' or to 'every man is unjust'.[1] For example, is 'Callias is just' contrary to 'Callias is not just' or to 'Callias is unjust'?[2]

Now if spoken expressions follow in accordance with corresponding *thoughts*, and if in *thought* a contrary opinion is of a contrary object—for example, if the opinion 'every man is just' is contrary to the opinion 'every man is unjust'—then a similar relation must exist between spoken affirmations also. But if, in *thought*, the contrary opinion is not of the contrary object, then the contrary of an affirmation will be its denial[3] and not the affirmation of the contrary object. So we must consider which true opinion is contrary to a false opinion,[4] whether the denial [of the false opinion] or the opinion of the contrary subject. What I mean is the following. There is a true opinion of a good thing, that it is good, and there is a false opinion of it, that it is not good, and still another [false][5] opinion of it, that it is bad. Which of the last two opinions is contrary to the true opinion? And if [the last two opinions are numerically] one [opinion],[6] in virtue of which one is [the true opinion] the contrary?

It is false to think that opinions should be defined as being contrary in view of the fact that they are opinions of contrary [subjects]. For the opinion of a good thing that it is good and the opinion of a bad thing that it is bad would be perhaps the same and be true, whether these opinions are more than one or just one.[7] The [subjects] here are contrary; but opinions are

contrary not by being of contrary [subjects], but rather by being contrary in
the manner in which they are related [to the same subject]. So if one opinion
of a good thing is that it is good and another that it is not good, and if there
are other things which neither belong nor are of such a nature as to belong
to a good thing, no opinion of those things should be posited [as being a
contrary opinion], whether it be an opinion of that which does not belong
to a good thing that it belongs to it or an opinion of that which belongs to
a good thing that it does not belong to it (for both kinds of opinions are
infinite, those of things which belong when they do not belong and those of
things which do not belong when they do belong), but only those in which
there is a mistake. Now these are opinions which arise from the generation
of things; but generations proceed from opposites, and so do mistakes.[8]
Accordingly, since a good thing is both good and not bad, since it is good
in virtue of its nature but is not bad in virtue of some attribute (for it is an
attribute of a good thing not to be bad),[9] and since an opinion is more true
of a thing if it is an opinion of it in virtue of its nature[10] [than if it is an
opinion not in virtue of its nature], an opinion will be more false of a thing
if it is false in virtue of the nature of that thing [than if it is false not in virtue
of the nature of that thing], as in the case of the true opinion.[11]

Now the opinion of a good thing that it is not good is false in view of what
belongs to the good thing in virtue of its nature, but the opinion of it that
it is bad is false in virtue of an attribute of that thing.[12] Hence the opinion
which denies that a good thing is good is more false than the opinion of the
contrary [i.e., the opinion of a good thing as being bad]. But the man whose
opinion is most false about a thing is he who has a contrary opinion, for
contraries are things which differ most concerning the same thing.
Accordingly, since only one of these two opinions is the contrary,[13] and since
the contradictory opinion[14] is more contrary than the other opinion [i.e.,
than the opinion that a good thing is bad], it is clear that the contradictory[15]
would be the contrary opinion. The opinion that a good thing is bad is
composite; for perhaps he who has this opinion must also believe that a good
thing is not good.[16] Further, if the situation is to be similar in the other cases
also, it would seem that in this way, too, we have given a good solution to
the problem; for the contradictory should be the contrary opinion either in
all cases or in none.[17] Now in [subjects] which have no contraries, there is a
false opinion which is opposed to the true. For example, he who thinks
falsely concerning a man is he who thinks that a man is not a man.[18] So if the
contrary opinions here are 'a man is a man' and 'a man is not a man', in the
other cases, too, the opinions which are contradictory[15] would be
contrary.

Again, the opinion of a good thing that it is good is similar to the opinion
of a thing which is not good that it is not good; and, we may add, the opinion
of a good thing that it is not good is similar to the opinion of a thing which

is not good that it is good.[19] Then which opinion would be contrary to the true opinion of a thing which is not good that it is not good? Certainly (a) not the opinion which thinks that it is bad, for both opinions might sometimes be true at the same time, and no true opinion is ever contrary to a true opinion (for [only] some things which are not good are bad, and so the two opinions might be true at the same time);[20] nor (b) the opinion that it is not bad, for this.opinion, too, might be true, since both 'not good' and 'not bad' might be predicable of a thing at the same time.[20] What remains, then, is that it is the opinion of a thing which is not good that it is good which is the contrary of the opinion of it that it is not good, for it is this opinion which is [always] a false opinion. So, too, it is the opinion of a good thing that it is not good which is the contrary of the opinion of it that it is good.

It is evident that it would make no difference even if we posited the affirmation to be universal, for in this case the contrary of it would be a universal denial. For example, the contrary of the opinion which thinks that everything which is good is good is the opinion that nothing which is good is good. For the opinion of a good thing that it is good, if a good thing is taken universally, is the same as the opinion that whatever is[21] good is good, and the latter opinion does not differ from the opinion that everything which is[21] good is good; and similarly with the opinions concerning what is not good.

So if indeed such is the case with opinions, since spoken affirmations and denials are symbols of the [corresponding] thoughts in the soul, it is clear that the contrary of an affirmation concerning something universally taken, too, is the corresponding denial universally taken; for example, the contraries of 'everything good is good' and of 'every man is good' are, respectively, 'nothing good is good' and 'no man is good', but the contradictories are, respectively, 'not everything good is good' and 'not every man is good'.

It is evident, too, that no true opinion or statement[22] can be contrary to a true opinion or statement, respectively. For contrary [opinions or statements] are of opposites; and whereas the same man may have true opinions or make true statements concerning two opposites, contraries cannot belong to the same [subject] at the same time.[23]

Commentaries

The references given in the Commentaries and in the Glossary are to the standard pages (sections) and lines according to Bekker's edition of Aristotle's works (Berlin, 1831). In particular, pages 1a1-24b9 cover the *Categories* and *On Propositions*, and these pages (and lines) appear as such in the margins of the translation. The Bekker pages covering each of Aristotle's works are as follows:

Categories: 1a1-15b33

On Propositions (De Interpretatione): 16a1-24b9.

Prior Analytics: 24a10-70b38.

Posterior Analytics: 71a1-100b17

Topics: 100a18-164b19

Sophistical Refutations: 164a20-184b8.

Physics: 184a10-267b26.

On the Heavens: 268a1-313b23.

On Generation and Destruction: 314a1-338b19.

Meteorology: 338a20-390b22.

On the Universe, To Alexander: 391a1-401b29.

On the Soul: 402a1-435b25.

On Sensation and Sensibles: 436a1-449a31.

On Memory and Recollection: 449b1-453b11.

On Sleep and Wakefulness: 453b11-458a32.

On Dreams: 458a33-462b11.

On Divination from Dreams: 462b12-464b18.

On Longevity and Shortness of Life: 464b19-467b9.

On Youth, Old Age, Life, and Death: 467b10-470b5.

On Respiration: 470b6-480b30.

On Breath: 481a1-486b4.

A Treatise On Animals: 486a5-638b37.

On Parts of Animals: 639a1-697b30.

On Motion of Animals: 698a1-704b3.

On Locomotion of Animals: 704a4-714b23.

On Generation of Animals: 715a1-789b20.
On Colors: 791a1-799b20.
On Objects of Hearing: 800a1-804b39.
Physiognomy: 805a1-814b9.
On Plants: 815a10-830b4.
On Reported Marvels: 830a5-847b10.
Mechanics: 847a11-858b31.
Problems: 859a1-967b27.
On Indivisible Lines: 968a1-972b33.
Positions and Names of Winds: 973a1-b25.
On Xenophanes, Zeno, and Gorgias: 974a1-980b21.
Metaphysics: 980a21-1093b29.
Nicomachean Ethics: 1094a1-1181b23.
Great Ethics: 1181a24-1213b30.
Eudemean Ethics: 1214a1-1249b25.
On Virtues and Vices: 1249a26-1251b37.
Politics: 1252a1-1342b34.
Household Management: 1343a1-1353b27.
Rhetoric: 1354a1-1420b4.
Rhetoric for Alexander: 1420a5-1447b7.
Poetics: 1447a8-1462b18.

Categories

1

1. An alternative translation is 'Things are said to be equivocal if . . .'. If so, then 'equivocal' would have the same meaning as 'having only a name in common'; and, with this meaning of the word, there is no logical difficulty in saying that things which are not names may be equivocal.

Linguistically, however, it seems strange to say that things are equivocal, for things are just what they are and do not equivocate, if we are to use 'equivocation' in the usual sense. Equivocation arises when a name is introduced and is used in different senses, so equivocation in this sense is an attribute primarily of names in relation to the things named and secondarily of things. Usually, Aristotle uses ὁμωνύμως λέγεται, which is translated as 'equivocally named', e.g., in 32a20, 110b16, 148a23, 1035bl, 1046a6, 1129a29 and in many other places, and this usage makes equivocation an attribute of names and not of the things signified by those names. Perhaps the word ὁμώνυμα is sometimes used as an adverb, and the word λέγεται rather than ἐστι in the first line seems to support this.

There is another alternative. If we are correct in our assumption that the *Categories* is an early work, and if the word ὁμώνυμα (= 'equivocal') as used here appears to be an attribute of things rather than of the corresponding names, then perhaps Aristotle changed his mind and used ὁμωνύμως (= 'equivocally') in his later works. Similar remarks apply to the words 'univocal' and 'derivative'.

The word for 'things' does not appear in the Greek, and a more literal expression would be: 'Those are named equivocally etc.'. So one may raise a logical problem, namely, whether equivocation applies to nonbeing as well as to being (or things), and hence whether the word 'things' should be included in the translation or not. To take an example, if 'number' is posited to mean number and also something impossible, like the square root of virtue, would the name 'number' be equivocally applied to four and to the object signified by 'the square root of virtue'? Four is a thing, but 'the square root of virtue' signifies nonbeing; so if equivocation applies to nonbeing also, then 'Objects are named equivocally etc.' should be the translation, for 'object' is posited to signify a being or nonbeing. Perhaps some definitions are needed to settle the problem.

Things which are equivocally named, we may add, may be closely related or may not. In Greek, a man and a medical instrument are equivocally called 'healthy', for this word means having health in the case of the man but producing health in the case of the instrument, but both the man and the instrument are related to health. The meanings of 'poker' when this name is applied to a game and to a rod used to stir a fire, on the other hand, have no close relation to each other. 249a23-5.

2. The word λόγος has many meanings, and here it means a set of words or names, like a statement. The word οὐσία is here translated as 'substance', and a synonym of 'substance' is 'essence', and sometimes 'nature' (1014b16-5a19, 1017b10-26). So the phrase ὁ λόγος τῆς οὐσίας signifies an expression of the *substance* of a thing, as in the statement 'a triangle is a three-sided plane figure'. But a definition is defined as a statement or an expression of the *substance* or essence of a thing; and it is a statement if it assumes a form such as 'a man is a rational animal', but an expression—also called 'definiens'—if it assumes a form such as 'a rational animal'. Consequently, the Greek phrase above, which we translate as 'the expression of the *substance*', may be translated as 'the definition' also. 90b16-7, 30-1, 101b39, 153a15-6, 154a31-2, 1031a11-4.

We often speak of the nature or essence of a thing, like the nature or essence of a triangle or of motion or of virtue or of man; and this nature is made known analytically through a definition. We shall retain the word '*substance*' for the sake of consistency in our translations.

Evidently, things which may be named equivocally are not limited to substances, which will be discussed later, but may be quantities or qualities or come under any of the other categories. 25b5, 1015a11-3, 1017b21-2, 1020a17-9, 1028b33-4.

3. The word γεγραμμένον may signify a picture or a painting or a work of sculpture, not necessarily of an animal; and it may even signify the word 'animal', which is not an animal.

4. Literally, the correct translation is 'an expression proper to each of them', which is an abbreviation of 'an expression of the *substance* proper to each of them', for Aristotle often abbreviates. But definitions proper to each of two different things are different definitions, and perhaps the expression 'a different definition' is easier to understand.

5. Does one borrow 'brave' from 'bravery', or conversely? Aristotle's primary concern here is philosophical, not linguistic. Accordingly, he considers a name which somehow signifies a composite as borrowed from a

name which signifies something simple. For example, 'brave' is predicable
of a composite, i.e., of a subject which has bravery, but 'bravery' is
predicable of bravery and not of any composite which includes a subject
and bravery. Bravery is a quality, but what we call 'brave' is usually a man
who has bravery, or else a virtuous *action* which we also call 'brave *action*'.
Similarly, 'white' is predicable of a body, which is a substance, and also of
a surface, which is a quantity; for a derivative name is not predicable of
substances only. 210b3-6, 1022a16-7.

2

1. Perhaps by 'not composite' he means an expression which signifies
one thing under one category, for the present discussion considers the
classification of things under general names or categories; and just as things
may be considered either singly or in combination, so may the
corresponding names. So since Aristotle's procedure here is scientific, his
first concern is to consider the principles and elements of a subject under
discussion. 184a10-6.

Incomposite expressions need not be one-word expressions. The
expressions 'triangle' and 'three-sided polygon' have the same meaning, and
each may be substituted for the other; so each should be considered as
incomposite. The Greek name for 'in the Lyceum' in 2a1 has two words, and
it is given as an example of an incomposite expression. Which expressions
of more than one word are incomposite? The discussion of this problem
belongs partly to metaphysics (1045a7-b23) and partly to grammar. It
appears, then, that an incomposite expression is one which signifies one
thing under one category, and if it is a verb, it adds time to the thing
(16b6-9).

Is the expression 'is brave' in 'Socrates is brave' composite or incomposite?
The examples used suggest that it is incomposite. For 'conquers' differs from
'is conquering' grammatically but not in meaning (20a3-7, 21b9-10), since
each signifies the same action; and just as 'conquers' is incomposite, so is 'is
brave'.

Perhaps the word λεγομένων should be translated as 'of things as
expressed', and in that case 'composite' would signify a combination not
necessarily of words but of two or more expressions each of which signifies
a thing in one category. If so, then 'in the Lyceum' would be incomposite,
and as for 'brave' in 'Socrates is brave', perhaps it signifies a certain relation,
namely, bravery as present in some subject, like 'double of three', which
signifies six in relation to three, or else, perhaps it signifies a subject related
in a certain way to bravery, as in 'the brave are virtuous'. Perhaps κατὰ
συμπλοκήν, too, should be translated as 'by composition', which is a more

literal translation. If so, then the sentence would begin as follows: 'Of things as expressed by composition'; and each part of a composite expression would be an expression signifying one thing under one category only. Further definitions could settle the matter.

2. The soul of some individual man is meant, e.g., the soul of Socrates and of no other, or the soul of Plato and of no other, not the whole soul but the thinking part of it, i.e., what one usually calls 'mind'; and the same applies to the body in which a particular whiteness is present. Each particular point of grammar or particular whiteness is taken as an individual with its own time, place, and subject in which it exists.

3. The technical expressions introduced here are 'said of' and 'present in', and they are stated as signifying certain relations (let us say, the said-of and present-in relations) between things, not necessarily of statements or of thoughts. These relations are very abstract and difficult to grasp, and some discussion concerning them may help the reader.

We assume that if A is present in B, it is not said of B, that if it is said of B, it is not present in B, and that if as a thing it belongs to B, it is either said of it or is present in it. Further, we assume that if A is said of B, B is not said of A, and that if A is present in B, B is not present in A. These statements will become clearer as the discussion proceeds. Let us begin with the present-in relation.

Let A and B be two individual men. A's particular color and particular shape are present in A but not in B or in any other individual man. If both A and B are sick, A's particular sickness is present in A but not in B, even if both suffer from the same kind of sickness. In general, A's individual attributes, which are not his nature or parts of his nature (a thing's nature is signified by its definition, e.g., by 'rational man' in the case of a man, and a part of that nature may be the genus or the differentia or a part of any of these), are present in A and in no other man or substance. Evidently, the individual attributes of A are not material parts, and so they cannot be separated (though they may be distinguished) from A in which they are present and be exhibited by themselves. A's bravery (if he is brave) or any other individual bravery cannot exist by itself, nor can the surface of any body.

An attribute of A, we may add, is never said of A; it is always present in A. Hence no attribute of A is the essence or a part of the essence of A, whether this part be a genus or a differentia. Such parts are said to be essential elements or essential parts of A. For example, rationality is not an attribute of man; it is an essential part of man.

Just as A's individual attributes are present in A, so we may truly say that, universally, an attribute is present in a substance, or attributes are present in substances, and that color is always present in a body, bravery is always present in a brave man or some other subject, and sickness is present only in a living thing. Further, if P is present in Q, Q need not be a substance; but P is ultimately present in a substance. For example, colors are present in surfaces of physical bodies (210b4-6, 1022a16-7), and these surfaces are present in these bodies, which are substances; hence colors are ultimately present in substances. As for properties, it appears that they are present in the things of which they are properties; for a property of a thing is not the nature or part of the nature of that thing but may be demonstrated to belong to that thing, and since it is not said of the thing, it must be present in it. For example, the equality of the three angles of a triangle to two right angles is a property of a triangle and so is present in a triangle.

Whether the expression 'color exists in a surface' is an abbreviation of 'each individual color exists in just one individual surface' is not clear. Perhaps the two statements as they stand do not mean the same thing; for the first is like the universal statement 'every man is mortal', and the truth of this statement is not limited by time or place, for it means that whenever and wherever a man exists, he is mortal. But the second statement may be ambiguous; for the word 'exists' in it may signify only the present, or it may signify potentially any time and any place.

Let A be present in B. Then we often use such expressions as 'A is in B', 'A belongs to B', 'A is an aspect of B', and 'B has A'; and when we say 'B is A', 'A' is usually a derivative term, as in 'Socrates is brave', for 'brave' is derived from 'bravery'. Linguistic expressions for the same thing vary, within the same language as well in different languages, and because of such variations men are often inclined to attribute corresponding differences to things when no such differences exist. Logically, the statements 'Socrates is a man' and 'Socrates has humanity' differ only linguistically.

The said-of relation is more difficult to grasp, for it is bound up with the nature of the universal; but we shall try to explain it as we understand it. If A is said of B, then A is the nature of B, or a part of that nature, and it is signified by the definition or a part of the definition of B. In the expression 'Socrates is an animal', for example, animal is said of Socrates. Other such expressions are 'this whiteness is a color', 'the Empire State is a building', 'a man is an animal', 'whiteness is a quality', 'a triangle is three-sided', 'a double is a multiple', and 'striking is acting'; and in each of these what is signified by the predicate is said of what is signified by the subject. In general, if A is a genus or a differentia or the species of B, then A is said of B; and if B is a substance, A is a substance or a differentia of a substance, if B is a quantity, A is a quantity or a differentia of a quantity, and similarly with the rest. In short, if B comes under a certain category, A comes under the same category, whether as a genus or a species or a differentia under that genus. Also, if A is said of B, then 'A is said of B' is true; for 'said of' is taken to signify not a saying or a statement which might be false, but a certain relation which exists between two things. Of course, we might misuse the expression, for we might say 'Socrates is said of Plato', which would be false; but we shall omit such expressions here.

Difficulties arise, however, with respect to that which is said of something else. If A is said of B, A is posited as being a thing and as somehow belonging to B. Is A one thing? But A is said of many things and would then belong to many things at the same time; for man is said of many men, and quantity is said of many of its species and of individual quantities. Is A a universal? What is a universal? Where and how does it exist? These and other related problems are not discussed in the *Categories*, for they belong to metaphysics or to some other science. On the other hand, if one is to be convinced of, or even understand, what is said in the *Categories*, some discussion of these difficulties is advisable; and, besides, even if no adequate solutions are forthcoming, still it is better to be aware of the difficulties than to be premature in our judgments concerning the truth or falsity of what is said there. First, then, we shall lay down what Aristotle says about the universal in general.

(1) The universal by its nature is predicable of or belongs to many. 17a39-40, 77a6-7, 644a27-8, 1038b11-6.

(2) The universal does not exist as something separate and apart from the many. 77a5-6, 85a31-5, 1038b30-3, 1040b26-7.

(3) That which is always and everywhere is said to be universal. 87b32-3, 96a8-9.

(4) The universal is not sensible but intelligible. 87b30-1.

(5) The universal is not a substance or a *this*; it is or signifies a *such*, or else a relation or a manner or something of this sort. 87b31, 178b37-9, 1003a8-9, 1038b8-9, 1038b35-9a2, 1087a2.

(6) The universal exists in the soul. 100a6-9, 15-6, 432a3-6.

(7) The universal, being one beside the many, is the same in all of them. 100a6-8.

The expressions 'A is said of B' and 'A is predicable of B' do not have the same meaning, although A is called 'a universal' in both of them, whether univocally or not. For in 2a19-27 it appears that what is predicable of something else may be an expression, which is either written or vocal, or it may be a thought in the soul, whereas what is said of a thing (which need not be an expression or a thought) apears to be different from an expression or a thought and to belong somehow to the thing of which it is said; for man in what is signified by 'Socrates is a man' is not an expression or a thought but something taken to belong somehow to Socrates, otherwise Socrates, in being a man, would be an expression or a thought also. Again the expression 'men are mortal' or 'every man is mortal', too, is said to be universal, and so is that which is signified by it, as is indicated by (3). It appears, then, that the name 'universal' applies to expressions or thoughts as well as to what they signify. But we are not concerned with the universal as an expression or as something in the soul as stated in (6); so let us leave this aside.

The universal as something separate was posited by Plato, and this is a Form or an Idea. As separate, it is one, a substance, eternal, immovable, and a model or pattern for the corresponding sensibles of which it is the cause. But as separate, it appears to be an individual, and Aristotle denies the existence of such an object. Most of Aristotle's criticisms against the existence of Ideas are in the *Metaphysics*.

If, in (5), the universal is not a *this*, does it signify a *such* or a relation or a manner or something of this sort, as stated in 178b37-9, where man (or the name 'man') is given as a universal? What would be a relation here might appear to be a name insofar as it signifies some other thing, but it is not clear how a name would signify a manner or something of this sort, unless a name other than 'man' is taken as a universal. On the other hand, another translation of καθόλου is 'universally', and perhaps this signifies the manner in which a thing such as man or the corresponding name 'man' functions with respect to that of which it is said or is predicable; for such a thing or name by its nature is said of or is predicable, respectively, of many. Here, of course, we are not concerned with the universal which is limited to a name.

For Aristotle, then, a universal which is said of something is (a) that which by its nature belongs or can belong to many, (b) that which does not exist by itself or as a primary substance, (c) that which does not exist apart from the many, (d) that which is not sensible but intelligible, (e) that which is one beside the many, and (f) that which is one and the same in all of them. Perhaps we can get some idea of what Aristotle means by 'a universal' by examining these six items.

Now a category (or any genus under it) is said of any of its species and of any individual under its species; and a differentia is likewise said of the species of which it is the differentia, of any lower species, and of any individual under that species. For example, animal or rational is said of man and of any individual man, and magnitude or continuous is said of a polygon and of a triangle and of an individual triangle. Since the relation signified by 'said of' is the same or similar in all categories, let us limit our discussion to the universal which is said of a specified substance, e.g., to animal, which is said of man and of an individual man.

(a) There seems to be no difficulty in believing and positing something common (i.e., a universal) which belongs by nature to many individuals. If individual men had nothing in common, there would be no point in calling each of them by the same name, e.g., by 'man' or 'animal'; and in general, each thing would be entirely different from any other thing and could be known only by sensation, and it could be signified only by one name, its own name, and be communicated verbally by another person only if it had been first sensed by both persons. Moreover, universal knowledge, such as 'every man is mortal' and 'two and two make four', would be impossible; and so would a syllogism, for a syllogism requires at least one universal premise (41b6-9, 77a5-9). The qualification 'by nature' is added because, though only one individual under a species may exist at a certain time, e.g., only one individual chair, or even no chair at all, many of them may also exist, and so chair as a universal may, by its nature, be said of many. Such an expression as 'square circle' or what it signifies, then, would not be a universal; for the expression 'square circle' signifies the kind of nonbeing which cannot exist and hence cannot be said of anything.

(b) There is no evidence whatsoever that a universal, such as man, exists by itself separately or as a primary substance does; and if one posits it so to exist, as Plato did, the difficulties and contradictions which would follow have been sufficiently pointed out in the *Metaphysics* and elsewhere.

(c) If the universal exists apart from the many of which it is said but not as something separate, perhaps it exists as a concept or a name. But a concept exists in the soul, and a name is vocal or written. Man and tree as universals, then, might exist as concepts; so since man has weight and redness is a color, a concept might have weight or be colored, and these consequences are absurd. Moreover, in the statement 'Socrates is a man', man (for Aristotle) is affirmed as belonging to Socrates and not to 'Socrates' as a concept, which is in the soul. Similarly, in 'this redness is a color', color is affirmed as belonging to an individual redness and not to the corresponding sensation, which is in the soul. It appears, then, that the universal does not exist as something which is apart from the many.

(d) Let us assume that the universal is sensible. Then if it is posited as one, it may be sensed as one but will not be said of or belong to many, and if it is posited as many, then in a statement such as 'Socrates is a man' Socrates will turn out to be many. If the universal is known at all, then, it cannot be sensible but, let us say, intelligible; for what is thought but is not sensed is said to be intelligible.

(e) As already stated, if man as a universal were many and not one, then Socrates would be many, for this would follow from the expression 'Socrates is a man' and from the assumption that man, which is a universal, is many. Moreover, the statement 'the universal is many' does not follow from the statement 'the universal is said of many'. What remains, then, is the difficult problem of understanding how that which somehow is one may be said of many.

(f) In the two statements 'Socrates is a man' and 'Plato is a man' man is said of two individuals, and the verb 'is' seems to indicate that man is in Socrates and in Plato somehow or belongs to both, who are two substances and who are separate. But can one and the same thing be in two separate things? If not, then perhaps man in Socrates differs in some way from man in Plato; but in what way? Would 'belonging to Socrates' be a predicate of man which is in Socrates but not of man which is in Plato? If so, then perhaps the particular time of existence and the particular place and other particulars would belong to man which is in Socrates also, and this is impossible; for particulars come and go, whereas man which is in Socrates is regarded as remaining constant or the same. But 'belonging to Socrates' seems to be always true of man which is in Socrates. On the other hand, if man which is in Socrates differs in some respect or respects from man which is in Plato, is man in these two the same in any respect at all? If not, we are faced with the diffculties discussed in (a); if yes, let S be that which is the same. But we are back to the same problem, for we have replaced man by S. For if S in Socrates differs from S in Plato in some respect, the process of seeking that which in Socrates and in Plato is the same and without any difference will go on to infinity, and from this it would follow that there is nothing which is the same and without any difference in Socrates and in Plato; but if the two S's do not differ in any respect, it would be reasonable to stop with man in the first place and conclude that man which is both in Plato and in Socrates (and also in others) is the same and without any difference.

The arguments for a universal which is one and the same but can exist in many without any difference at all when said of them are so far logical. Perhaps a different approach is also advisable. The word 'one', and likewise for the word 'same', has many senses; and in one sense it means one in species (1016b31-33, 1018a4-6, 1052a32-3). Both Socrates and Plato come under the species man, and both are indistinguishable insofar as each is a man. In other words, whether one abstracts and forms the concept of man by attending to Socrates or to Plato makes no difference, for all other things which belong to Socrates or to Plato not as men are excluded from man and hence from the concept of man. Man as something in Socrates is exactly the same as (or similar to, if you wish) man in Plato, and because of this relation of sameness in the two, one can form just one concept of man. This relation of sameness between things is a fact in things and a principle, and without it universal knowledge and communication would be impossible. In saying that Plato and Socrates are one in species or the same in species or are men or something of this sort, then, one means that man in the two of them is indistinguishable and hence that one can have only one concept of man. Man, then, is one in the sense that man is one in kind or species and is conceived as the same in individual men and so is indistinguishable as a nature, and from this it follows that one can have only one concept and only one definition of man. Men are many, on the other hand, not just by being each a man but by having attributes which differ from one individual man to another and which may change for each of them, for men differ by having different individual places and other individual attributes. Hence there can be no single definition of an individual as an individual, for such a definition would be changing from moment to moment.

If A is said of B, we have stated that A is ultimately said of an individual, say of Z. If A is in the category of substance, whether it be a genus or a species or a differentia, Z is a substance also, and neither A nor B nor Z is present in any other thing. But if A is in some other category, all three of them (A, B, and Z) are also present in something else. For example, magnitude is said of surface, and surface is said of a particular surface; and magnitude is present in a particular body, which is a substance, and so is surface, and a particular surface is present in a particular body.

An individual (male) man should be regarded as having man or the nature of man not in the same sense as he has sickness or a dress or a wife; for in the latter sense he can exist as an individual man without sickness or a dress or a wife, whereas in the former he cannot do so, since without his nature he no longer exists. Hence an individual man should be regarded not as a subject or a substratum without any attributes or any nature, but as something which is a nature and has also attributes, whether these attributes are always present or not; for to regard him as a subject without anything yet receptive of other things is to regard him as prime matter, which is an underlying principle but has, *as such*, neither a nature nor any attribute under any of the categories, and this is not Aristotle's position (1029a20-1). We may add, it is literally more true to say that an individual substance is a nature than to say that it has a nature; for if 'B' is not a derivative name in 'A is B', B is an essential part of A, as in 'Socrates is a man', but B in 'A has B' need not be an essential part of A, as in 'Socrates has sickness'.

A difficulty arises with species. Since Socrates is a man, and a man is a species, Socrates appears to be a species. The name 'species', of course, has two senses (see next Commentary's second paragraph): (a) that which is said of a thing, as man of Socrates, and (b) that which is predicable of a thing or a name, as 'man' is predicable of Socrates or of 'Socrates'. Evidently, Socrates is not a name. If species is taken as the nature of a thing, or as that which is in the nature of the thing coming under that species, then it is that which can be said also of many things like that thing. If so, then to say that Socrates is a species is to say that Socrates is that which can be said also of many things like Socrates; and there is nothing strange about this.

Let this be our understanding of things which are said of other things or are present in them.

The Greek word *ἐν*, translated here as 'present in', has other meanings also.

3

1. If A is predicable of B, A appears to be a name, whether written or vocal, or even a concept in the soul; but it is not clear whether 'predicable

of' is so used that B itself is a name. For example, is the name 'animal' predicable of man or of 'man' or of both, of Socrates or of 'Socrates' or of both? Lines 2a19-27 suggest that B is not a name; but no quotation marks appear in the Greek text, and this presents a problem for the reader. The same problem arises with respect to the name 'subject'; for if B must be a name, then 'subject' has two meanings, one for names, i.e., for grammatical subjects (but not all of them), and another for what these signify. The expression 'as of a subject' and line 2a19 later appear to distinguish 'predicable of' from 'said of' and from 'present in' but do not specify whether B must be a name or not. We have so translated the Greek text that a subject may be either a thing or a name, but there is a limitation. In the expression 'A is predicable of B, and B is predicable of C', if C is not a name, then either both B's are names, in which case B is used univocally, or the first B is a thing but the second B is the name which signifies that thing, in which case B is used equivocally. In the second case, for example, 'animal' is predicable of man, and 'man' of Socrates.

Similar problems arise with respect to the names 'genus', 'species', 'universal' and other allied names, for 'species' may signify, to take an example, either man or the name 'man'. Since a genus is predicable of a species of it according to line 1b22, it appears that 'genus' may signify a name or a thing which is not a name.

In the first sentence of this paragraph there appears a difficulty, which is perhaps linguistic. If 'said of' is to have the meaning already indicated, then either 'the predicate' should signify a thing but not a name, or 'said of the predicate' should have the same meaning as 'predicable of the predicate', and 'said of the subject' should have the same meaning as 'predicable of the subject'; otherwise, there would be an inconsistency. The example given fits both alternatives, the first indirectly (for if A is said of B, then 'A' is predicable of B or of 'B') but the second directly. Perhaps Aristotle is using 'said of' in more than one sense, one of them applying to things, another to names.

The phrase 'for an individual man is both a man and an animal' indicates that the relation of being predicable follows from the said-of relation, but not conversely, for truth is somehow caused by what exists, but not conversely. 14b9-22.

Concerning the name 'subject', if B is said of A or is present in A, then A is the subject of B in the sense that A is B (or a B) or has in itself B, and the relation between A and B is close (or natural, if you wish). But if B is a name and is predicable of the name A or of what A signifies, no such close relation exists, except by convention; for A is not B when we truly say 'B is predicable of A', and B is not present in A. For example, the name 'animal' is not said of the name 'man', and the name 'whiteness' is not present in the name 'Socrates' if Socrates is white. Perhaps it is in view of this difference that Aristotle uses 'as of a subject' in line 1b10; for A in the statement 'B is predicable of A' acts like a subject in the first sense by signifying a subject and not by being a subject in that sense.

Literally, the word κατηγορεῖσθαι should be translated as 'to be predicated'; but we are translating it as 'to be predicable', for if a man actually predicates A of B and B of C, A is predicable of C even if one does not actually predicate A of C. Perhaps a definition of κατηγορεῖσθαι would settle the matter.

In saying that 'A' is predicable of 'B', we may add, it is assumed that 'B is A' is true.

For Aristotle, the relations signified by 'present in', 'said of', and 'predicable of' are transitive, but modern logicians object to this transitivity when they say that Aristotle fails to distinguish, for example, between predicating a genus of a species and predicating a species or a genus of an individual. The objection, however, has no force. Although the above distinction exists, it does not affect the transitivity of these relations; for 'all A is B' does not have the same meaning for Aristotle as for modern logic. This will be considered in Comm. 7 of Section 5 and discussed in detail later in the treatise *On Propositions*.

2. Both animals and plants are living things, and the differentiae of living things (i.e., growth, taking in food, reproduction, etc.) are differentiae of both plants and animals. But the subdivision of animals into further species gives rise to differentiae which cannot be differentiae of plants or of things which are not animals. So it is a mark of a differentia under a genus G that it is not predicable of things which do not come under G.

3. Since a right triangle is a polygon, and a polygon is a many-sided plane surface, a right triangle, too, is many-sided and plane; hence 'many-sided' and 'plane' are predicable of that triangle, or of any species of a triangle. A right triangle, we may add, has additional differentiae.

4

1. An alternative translation of this sentence up to here is: 'Of expressions of things which are not composite, each signifies.' See Comm. 1, Section 2.

2. Alternatives to 'a quantity', 'a quality', and 'a relation' are 'quantified', 'qualitative', and 'relative', respectively. The Greek names here (i.e., ποσόν, ποιόν, etc.) are used sometimes as nouns and sometimes as adjectives, and when used like adjectives they appear to be derivative names. Sometimes Aristotle uses alternative names which can function only as nouns; e.g., he uses the nouns ποσότης (= 'quantity') in 1028a19 and

ποιότης (= 'quality') in 8b25 and 1020a19. The adjective, of course, signifies also an implied subject, not necessarily a substance, in which the attribute indicated by the adjective is present. For example, 'virtuous' signifies also a subject, e.g., a man or an *action*, in which virtue is present.

A problem still remains. Does Aristotle use the names which signify things other than substances as adjectives or as nouns? An adjective in a category other than substance, e.g., 'virtuous' or 'great', appears to signify either (a) an implied subject in which the attribute specified by the adjective is present, or (b) a specified attribute with the indication that it is present in a subject. Now in Section 6, on quantity (4b20), the word ποσόν seems to be used as a noun, for 'number', 'body', 'surface' and the other names which are used as species of ποσόν are nouns. In the Sections on relation and quality there are arguments for both positions. I am inclined to think that the names are used as nouns, for in this way an analysis of statements of facts and relations between kinds of things lessens the possibility of confusion.

3. We translate the Greek word κεῖσθαι as 'being in a position', which is taken as a genus of 'lying', 'standing', 'sitting', etc.

4. Each of these expressions is a translation of a single word in Greek.

5. From one manuscript, the translation would be 'cutting' and 'burning' instead of 'cuts' and 'burns', and 'being cut' and 'being burned' instead of 'is cut' and 'is burned'. The infinitive, however, is not necessary, for 'cuts' is an instance or an example of 'cutting', and similarly for the others.

6. The problem of whether the categories (or the most general classes of things, if you wish) are ten or some other number is a matter of induction and intuition. Difficulties arise, however, with respect to some of those listed, and they will be raised as each of the categories is taken up in the text. One may arrive at them by asking various kinds of general questions. What? Where? When? What kind? How much? One may also arrive at them by taking, let us say, a surface and asking 'What is it?' till he arrives at the ultimate genus, quantity, which is a category. But these are dialectical procedures; for one must have the intuition of a category *as such* before answering generically the corresponding question, e.g., one must have an intuition of quantity *as such* before stating analytically that this is so-much of a quantity, or that it is a quantity. By saying 'a given thing is a line three feet long' or 'three is a number', a man does not necessarily have the concept of quantity, for this concept is acquired from that line or from number by further abstraction.

By 'category' we shall mean either an ultimate genus as a name, e.g., 'quantity', or what that name signifies.

5

1. This statement is not a definition of a substance as a category but only a sort of dialectical explanation, or else a property; for a category has neither a genus nor a differentia (1014b9-10), and hence it cannot be defined. A further indication of this is the fact that the statement states what a substance is not, not what it is; but a definition states what a thing is, not what it is not.

The three key terms 'most fundamental', 'primary', and 'highest sense' deserve comment. From 2b37-3a1, 76a16-8, 123a34-6, 981b9-11, and 1143b33-5 it appears that A is fundamental to B (and B is dependent on A) if B's existence or knowledge or action depends on that of A, but A's existence or knowledge or action, respectively, does not depend on that of B. Here, the dependence seems to be one of existence. Now while all attributes depend on substances if they are to exist (and also if they are to be known, 1028a34-6, 1045b30-2), secondary substances, too, depend on primary substances for their existence. So 'most fundamental' is used here to imply also the dependence of secondary substances for their existence on primary substances. Accordingly, we are using the words 'dependent' and 'fundamental' as contraries and not as contradictories, unless otherwise indicated. Hence if A is fundamental to B, then B is dependent on A. The contradictory of 'dependent', then, would be 'not dependent', and the contradictory of 'fundamental' would be 'not fundamental'; hence that which is not dependent on M need not be fundamental to M.

Another English name for 'primary' is 'first', and primary substances are first in a number of ways. Being fundamental to all others, primary substances are first in existence; and in underlying all other things, even secondary substances, they are first as subjects (1019a4-6). They are also first as final causes, as in individual men, and perhaps in other ways.

The expression 'highest sense' is the superlative of 'more'. Both expressions are used mainly or mostly for qualities (10b26-11a14), as when one thing is said to be more white or more virtuous or more curved than another. They are also used to relate things other than qualities (2b7-8, 6b20-7), but whether they are univocally so used or equivocally, is not clear. Perhaps a primary substance is more complete or more perfect in some way than a secondary substance. A secondary substance is certainly more perfect than a genus of it, for it has a differentia which is lacking in the genus; and the species of a primary substance has more *actuality* than a genus of it, for it is more definite and indicates the nature of a primary substance more than a genus of it does.

2. Primary and secondary substances exclude each other, and their difference appears to be clear; but a difficulty arises. Since Socrates is a man and man is a secondary substance, Socrates would appear to be a secondary

substance, contrary to the fact that he is a primary substance. We do not know Aristotle's solution, if he had any, but we may venture one of our own.

If a primary substance is primary insofar as it has accidents, and if a secondary substance is secondary insofar as it has no accidents, then Socrates insofar as he is primary is not a secondary substance; for man, being a secondary substance, has no accidents. This is also evident from the fact that Socrates is a man not insofar as he has accidents. Thus both primary and secondary substances are substances if no reference is made to accidents, and the two kinds, though not species of substance, are exclusive.

3. Evidently, a name is predicable of a thing because what is signified by the name is said of the thing, but if A is said of B, it is not because the name 'A' is predicable of B. It is like a truth and the fact it signifies. Each implies the other, but the fact is somehow the cause or a cause of the truth, whereas the truth is not the cause or a cause of the fact. 14b9-23.

4. Aristotle is often incomplete, if not careless, in his statements; and here we have added the bracketed expression for the sake of the reader. It is possible, however, that he is using the word κατηγορεῖσθαι (= 'to be predicable') in two senses. Other places in the *Categories* in which that which is predicable appears to be not a name but the thing signified by the name are 2b16, 31, 3a4, 38, b2, 12a1, 7, 14, 16, 40, b29.

5. In the Greek (as in English) the name corresponding to 'white' is used as an adjective as well as a noun, and hence in two senses. As a noun, 'white' means whiteness, and the corresponding definition of white will be the definition of whiteness; and just as we do not say 'man is whiteness', so we do not use the definition of whiteness instead of that of white in 'man is white'. There are few names which are used in two such senses, and this is the reason for the phrase 'in most cases' in the first sentence of this paragraph. Thus, if 'A' is predicable of B but is not used as a derivative name in that predication, then in most cases A and B come under the same category, but if they do not, the reason is linguistic and does not depend on the fact signified. See also Comm. 12.

If the definition of white as a composite of a subject and whiteness is used in 'man is white', it appears that no difficulty would arise. But what would the genus in that definition be? The subject may be a substance, e.g., a man, or it may be a quantity, for whiteness is present in a surface, and quantities and substances have nothing in common as natures. Further, a definition according to Aristotle is limited to a thing under one category and does not apply to composites, except in a qualified way. 1029b1-1030b13.

6. One would expect Aristotle to say 'animal is said of man' here, for it appears that he is considering things which are either said of primary substances or are present in primary substances. Perhaps he argues dialectically from the manner in which we speak to the way in which things

exist. Anyway, the word 'predicable' here signifies the said-of relation. Usually, as stated in 2a27-31, if 'A' is predicable of B, then A is said of B.

Similar remarks apply to lines 2b15-8.

7. This paragraph indicates how Aristotle uses the verb 'is' in 'all A is B' with respect to existence. If individual men do not or cannot exist, then 'all men are animals' will be false for Aristotle; and if so, then 'some men are animals' follows from 'all men are animals', for the word 'are' in the two statements is used univocally and not equivocally. For modern logic, on the other hand, 'some A is B' does not follow from 'all A is B'; for 'is' in 'all A is B' means: for every x, if x is an A, then it is also a B, but in 'some A is B' the word 'is' is not used conditionally, for 'some A is B' means: there exists an A which is also a B. Thus if there exists no x which is an A, then 'some A is B' is false; but 'all A is B' is true, for the falsity of 'all A is B' depends only partly on the existence of an x which is an A. Any criticism against Aristotle's position, then, has to rest on principles which are not logical, e.g., on such principles as adequacy and value.

An objection might be raised. If a universal name is by nature predicable of many (1038b11-2), then for Aristotle 'every A is B' may be true potentially though not actually, as in 'all houses are white' when no house exists at time T but may exist later and be white. On the other hand, potential existence may apply to 'some A is B' as well, or to 'A_1 is B', where A_1 is an individual, so the objection seems to lose its force. For, if A_1 does not exist now, 'A_1 is B' may be potentially and also vacuously true; for one may take 'A_1 is B' to mean that if A_1 exists, then A_1 is B. But does Aristotle give different meanings to 'is' in the two statements 'A_1 is A' and 'every A is B'? From *Prior Analytics*, 34b7-18, it is clear that he does not, for he posits that the meaning of 'to belong' (or of the word 'is', if you wish) is taken without qualification (that is, uniformly the same), though he allows for qualifications if need arises.

8. The syllogism goes as follows. A species is more informative and more appropriate to the whatness of a primary substance than a genus of it; that which is more informative and more appropriate to a primary substance is closer to it; that which is closer to it is a substance to a higher degree; hence a species of a primary substance is to a higher degree a substance than a genus of it.

9. If the name 'white' or 'runs' is used to describe a man, one would not know that the thing described is a man, for 'runs' is predicable of many animals, and 'white' is predicable also of some inanimate bodies and of certain colors. Besides, whiteness and running are accidental to man or to animals, for a man or an animal need not be white or running; but a man must be a man and an animal, and 'animal' and 'man' are necessary predicates of him and also close to him.

10. If 'these' signifies all other things except primary substances, then 'predicable' would seem to signify the names corresponding to all things other than primary substances. Perhaps 'these' excludes also individuals and their names, for while an individual (e.g., an individual quality) is present in an individual belonging to some species or genus, it is not present in that species or genus as in a whole. As for a predicate such as 'grammatical', which is universal, though predicable of an individual man who is grammatical, it is not predicable of the whole species of men; but if predicable at all, it would be predicable of men, for 'some men are grammatical' would be true. Perhaps it is in this sense that, if an individual man is grammatical, 'man is grammatical' is true, as is stated in what follows; for 'man is grammatical' is indefinite and is not the same as 'all men are grammatical', and whether some men or all men are grammatical, 'man is grammatical' is true. Evidently, if 'man is grammatical' is true, so is 'animals are grammatical'. Indefinite statements such as 'man is white' (or 'men are white') are taken up in the treatise *On Propositions*.

11. The distinction between an attribute of a thing and the essence or nature of that thing must be kept in mind. Now 'man' signifies the nature and 'animal' signifies part of the nature of an individual man, but what Aristotle calls 'an attribute of a thing' is not the nature of a thing or a part of that nature, although the attribute belongs to the thing, whether always, like a property, or sometimes, like an accident. Correspondingly, it is the nature or part of the nature of a thing that is said of but is not present in that thing, and what is present in but not said of a thing is something other than the nature or part of the nature of that thing, and this is called 'an attribute' and belongs to the thing. Evidently, man is not present in a thing which is not a substance, whether that thing is an individual or a universal, for no substance belongs to a non-substance; but to man are present such things as quantity, quality, and the rest. In a certain sense, then, non-substances are parts of substances (not material parts, for the word 'part' has many senses, 1023b12-25), but not conversely, and no substance can be present in a non-substance.

12. As stated in Commentary 5, the name 'white' has two meanings, namely, a certain color and also a subject with that color, and 'white' is predicable of a white surface or body. There are few such names, and this is brought out by the word 'sometimes' in line 3a16. Now 'white' is predicable of a white man, but the definition of white as a color is not predicable of him, for he is not a color of any sort. What about the definition of white as a subject with whiteness? For one thing, whiteness and the subject in which it is present form a composite and not a single thing in a single category; for another, there can be no definition of such a composite, for a definition is of one thing only (17a13-5, 1029b1-31a14), and here we are concerned with relations between things each of which may come under

a different category. The only thing that can be defined determinately in what is signified by 'white' as a derivative name is whiteness, for the subject may be either a surface, which is a quantity, or a body, which is a substance. Of course, one may use 'definition' in another sense and so define whatever he pleases. According to Aristotle, the discussion of the nature of definition belongs mainly to metaphysics, for definitions are not limited to any special science but appear in all sciences.

13. But is not 'rational', which is a part of the definition of man or an individual man, a name signifying a quality, or a derivative name derived from 'rationality'? If so, 'human' and 'man' would likewise be derived from 'humanity' and 'manhood' (or 'manness'), and also 'animal' from 'animality', and similarly for all others, whether names have been coined or not. But animality and humanity are not present in anything; for if they were, similar remarks would apply also to the things they would be present in and to their names, and this would go on to infinity. Thus it appears that the arguments for a difference between animal and animality and others of this sort depend on linguistic or grammatical usage and not on the things themselves; for the distinctions into categories still exist, and so do the said-of and present-in relations as indicated, and we should not be misled by the adjectival form of 'rational'. In fact, there is only one Greek word for the two names 'two-footed' and 'two-footedness', namely, πεζόν, and this is the case for many others. It appears, then, that though the genus and the differentia of a species differ as parts of that species, it is because they are both parts of the nature of the species that they are both said of that species and of the individuals under that species.

The relation between whiteness and man, then, is not the same as that between rational (or rationality) and man, for in the latter case the rational is a part of man's nature but the white (or whiteness) is not; and, in view of this distinction, the two different relations, said-of and present-in, still stand. The relation between the differentia and the genus of man appears to be in some sense analogous to that between man and an individual man; for just as 'man' appears to signify a sort of quality or kind of a certain primary substance, i.e., of an individual man (3b13-23), so 'rational' appears to signify a sort of quality or kind of the secondary substance animal (1020a33-b1).

14. The name 'part' has many senses (1023b12-25), and here a material part is meant, e.g., a hand or a foot of an individual man. Now such a part is separable, for it may be cut off, but the wisdom or the color of Socrates cannot be separated from him, though it may be distinguished from him.

15. Perhaps the meaning is as follows. A secondary substance or a differentia of it is said of a thing but is never present in a thing; hence the corresponding name cannot be derivatively predicated of that thing. Virtue

is present in the soul and Socrates is derivatively called 'virtuous', but there is no derivative name corresponding to 'man' or 'rational'; and we have already discussed (in Comm. 13) the difficulties in positing 'rational' and 'rationality' as having different meanings. Thus the word 'univocally' is used in contrast to 'derivatively' and not in contrast to 'equivocally'.

16. To be predicable of something, the name 'Socrates' has to appear in such a statement as 'X is Socrates', in which Socrates is present in or said of X. But this statement does not signify that Socrates is either said of X or is present in X, for this would be false; and we are concerned only with predications which signify a relation of said-of or of present-in. The above predication is called 'accidental', if true at all, and its discussion belongs to another inquiry. 43a25-36, 81b24-9.

17. Perhaps 'predicable' is more accurate than 'said'.

18. Aristotle does not define 'a *this*'. Perhaps he uses it dialectically to mean something which is obviously a whole of some sort, one, sensible, separate, easily recognizable and distinguishable from other things, and something which we can point to as when we say 'this object is so-and-so'; and such an object, of course, would be a primary substance but stated in a sort of popular way.

19. The name 'man' appears to signify one individual and hence a primary substance, but this is not the case since the name is predicable of many. It is not like the name 'Socrates', which signifies definitely and only one thing and is predicable of one thing only.

20. A thing is called 'much' or 'great' when it is related to other things of its kind and is not determinate, for what is great may be a foot long, like a cucumber, or a hundred yards high, like a tree; so it appears that greatness and smallness and other such things are relations. These are discussed in 5b11-6a11, and relations in general are discussed in 6a36-8b24.

21. Literally, the translation should be 'no substance is thought to admit of the more or the less'. The words 'more' and 'less' are used primarily for qualities but sometimes, in the absence of corresponding Greek words, perhaps analogously for different kinds of substances or things in other categories.

22. Secondary substances which vary in generality admit of variation of degree. 2b7-28.

23. An alternative to '*as such*' is 'insofar as it is a certain kind of'. See Comm. 2 of Section 7.

24. While the species man is more of a substance than the genus animal (perhaps using 'more' in an analogous sense, as indicated in Comm. 21), one man is not more of a man than another man or than himself at a different time insofar as he is just a man. The English expression 'he is more of a man' is used metaphorically.

25. This mark applies only to primary substances, for secondary

substances do not admit of contraries. In the case of secondary substances, one may raise a problem; for it is possible for all men to be healthy at one time and sick at another time, and so it would appear that man as a secondary substance admits of variation of degree. But the expression 'numerically one' limits the things of which it is predicable to primary substances, and perhaps to their lowest species; but secondary substances and other things do not, *as such*, admit of contraries. For example, five, which is a quantity, is odd but cannot be even, and no species which is not a genus of other species admits, *as such*, of contraries.

26. Contraries cannot exist in a thing at the same time and in the same respect, e.g., an individual man cannot be hot and cold at the same time, though part of him may be hot and part cold (in which case he is not hot and cold, but partly hot and partly cold); so if an individual thing is to admit of contraries at different times, it must be capable of changing. Now only material substances can change, e.g., men and trees and other such individual things which have movable matter. Things other than primary substances do not have movable matter and so cannot change; hence they cannot admit of contraries in themselves, whether at the same time or at different times. 5b39-6a3, 224b11-3, 1069b3-17.

27. A statement or an opinion is related to the object of which it is a statement or an opinion by signifying it. If the object is a fact, what signifies it is true; if the object is nonbeing (i.e., not a fact), what signifies it is false. If the object in virtue of its potentiality changes from a fact to nonbeing, then the statement which signifies that object as a fact changes from being true to being false, and if the object changes from nonbeing to a fact, then the statement signifying that object as a fact changes from being false to being true. Thus statements and opinions are true or false by being related to certain objects, and they change not in virtue of themselves but in virtue of the objects to which they are related. For example, the statement 'Socrates is sick' changes from being true to being false only if Socrates changes from being sick to being healthy, and Socrates has the potentiality of changing from being sick to being healthy.

28. A thing is said to change in an unqualified way if it is itself that changes, as in the case of a body which moves; but it is said to change in a qualified or accidental or indirect way if it changes not in this manner, as in the case of a statement which changes in the manner indicated in the preceding Commentary.

29. The expression 'being the same and numerically one' limits substances to primary substances, and each such substance must be the same, i.e., it must retain its nature. For example, Socrates must remain Socrates when changing from healthy to sick, and likewise for water when changing from hot to cold. 188a19-192b4, 999b33-4, 1018a25-35.

6

1. The subdivision of quantities into continuous and discrete is kept in the *Metaphysics*, 1020a10-2. Whether the parts of a number have a relative position to each other or not is partly a matter of how number is conceived and defined. The arithmetician is not concerned with relative position, so his definition of a number leaves position out. And if a particular number has parts which have relative position, as in the case of five men, although that position may vary as the men move about, the number as defined is not affected at all, for the arithmetician as arithmetician is not concerned with that position.

Do units exist? Whether what we call 'a unit' is indivisible or just undivided makes no difference; units as things exist in both senses. An individual man is indivisible with respect to his nature as a man, for there is no such thing as one-half or one-third of a man, and to speak of the square root of a man or the square of a man is ridiculous; and if he is undivided but divisible, it is qua a body, which is geometrical, that he is divisible and not qua a nature. Consequently, if the parts of what one regards as a number are studied as magnitudes with position, they are studied *as such* in geometry and not in arithmetic. Moreover, since the arithmetician studies units only universally, and since units *as such* do not differ with respect to quantity or quality (1083a1-4) or perhaps with respect to any other category, neither can they be related to each other in different ways; hence touching and being apart, which are contrary relations in geometry, do not belong to units, and so they do not come under arithmetic.

Now some things may be studied by more than one science, but in different respects; and two sciences may be so related that one of them presupposes the other. As a unit, a man is studied in arithmetic, as a certain nature with a purpose, he is studied in politics, and as a physical body, he is studied in physics. On the other hand, arithmetic presupposes logic, and harmonics presupposes arithmetic; in fact, astronomy, optics, mechanics, harmonics, and all sciences which nowadays come under what we call 'mathematical physics' are composite sciences and presuppose *knowledge* of logic and arithmetic and geometry. In general, the less abstract presupposes the more abstract. A more detailed account of these facts is given in *Posterior Analytics* and elsewhere.

Problems arise with respect to the name 'discrete'. Is it the contrary of 'continuous' or the contradictory? Again, is it a differentia of a number or just an explanation for the sake of the reader?

The name 'discrete' is the contrary and not the contradictory of 'continuous', and it is not a synonym of 'not continuous', which is the contradictory of 'continuous'. With very few exceptions, differentiae are formed not by negation but by adding further positive information to the genus (143b11-32); for it is in this manner that properties belonging to the things with such differentiae are investigated. For example, if 'equal-sided' is one differentia of a triangle, 'not equal-sided' cannot be another differentia of it; for what is not equal-sided need not be a triangle (e.g., man is *not* equal-sided), and if property P were to belong to a triangle insofar as it is not equal-sided, it would have to belong also to a man insofar as he is not equal-sided. But it is impossible for a property such as P to belong also to a man, for P would not be a property of a triangle. So while 'unequal-sided' or 'scalene' is a differentia of a triangle, 'not equal-sided' is not; for what is not equal may not be unequal (51b25-8). The name 'discrete', then, is the contrary of 'continuous' and should be understood as that contrary, and it applies to a quantity having parts each of which is by its nature indivisible. 1020a7-32.

2. The English translations use the word 'number' for ἀριθμός, and we shall retain the word 'number'; but the word ἀριθμοίς means a whole number or a cardinal number greater than 1 and should be understood as such. Accordingly, it would be unfair to say, as some do, that Aristotle had a limited concept of number, for matters of definition or convention are not matters of fact. The Greek word which is closest in meaning to what we mean by 'number' is ποσόν, which we translate as 'quantity'.

3. Usually, the word στερεόν is used (5a23), which we translate as 'solid', but sometimes Aristotle uses the word σῶμα, which we translate as 'body' and which usually means a physical body but sometimes a mathematical object which we call 'solid'.

4. The inclusion of speech as discrete quantity different from a number, and of time and place as additional kinds of continuous quantities, suggests that the *Categories* was written before the *Physics*, the *Posterior Analytics*, and the *Metaphysics*. See Commentaries 6, 7, and 8.

5. Some metaphysical questions may be raised concerning a number. If the parts have no common boundary or relative position, how can a number be one thing rather than many, and how can its units, which are regarded as parts, exist potentially rather than in *actuality*? If the units are separate from each other, they seem to exist in *actuality* and not as parts, and the addition of units or numbers to each other appears unnecessary. But if this is so, arithmetic as a science appears to be impossible.

Again, if the unity of a number depends on us, as when we number five objects and regard these taken together as possessing a unity, then the form of such a number is not in the number itself but depends on us; but the form of a thing is thought to be in the thing itself and not outside of it, e.g., the form of a given table is in that table and not outside of it (209b22-3).

According to 1016b6-9, "most things are called 'one' in view of the fact that they act on, or are affected by, or have, or are related to some other thing which is one", and perhaps a number is one in some one of these senses, but "things which are primarily called 'one' are those whose *substance* is one, either by continuity, or in kind, or in formula." Thus a line six feet long is primarily one by being continuous as a magnitude, but it is one as a number—six feet—by being related in a certain way to that line as a magnitude, i.e., by having six foot-units as parts which are one by continuity. If so, then perhaps five men, too, by being related to some one thing, e.g., by being the parts or members of a club, or by being in a room, or by being brothers, make up a number, which is one thing; for a club is one thing, and so is the room, and likewise for the father or mother or parents. If so, then addition is possible, and so is subtraction and the rest, for it is possible to point out some one thing in virtue of which a sum is one; but the arithmetician need not be concerned with the cause of that unity or with the properties which follow from that cause, or with these problems in general, for the senses of 'one' and the discussion of unity belong to the philosopher and not to the arithmetician, and the properties which follow from the cause of unity do not belong to arithmetic. For example, if that cause is continuity, the properties of continuity belong to geometry.

6. Speech is not mentioned in the *Metaphysics* (1020a7-32) as discrete quantity or as a quantity at all; and the mention of long and short syllables as units or measures suggests two kinds of units or measures, contrary to Aristotle's later position that units do not differ, insofar as they are just units, with respect to quantity or quality (1083a1-17). Units do differ as natures just as the senses of 'being' differ (1052a15-4a19), but such differences do not appear in arithmetic or in any mathematical science because the objects of these sciences are abstracted from such differences. Speech, then, would be a quantity not in virtue of itself but in virtue of an accident or indirectly, like the white, the musical, time, and motion (1020a26-32).

7. Elsewhere, the word 'time' appears to have two meanings for Aristotle; for, in one sense, time is continuous (220a4-5), in another, it is a number of motion (219b1-2, 220a3-4). But in both senses time is a quantity not in virtue of itself like a number or a line, but in virtue of something else (1020a26-32), for it depends on motion, and motion depends on a moving body, which has quantity. Here, however, time is regarded as continuous only; and 'present time' signifies not a moment, which is a limit of time and has no duration, but time as a continuous quantity with some duration. Present time, then, has two limits or moments, one of which joins a limit of the past and the other a limit of the future. But is present time a boundary?

8. Place, too, is like time. In the *Physics* (211b9-14, 212a5-6) it is defined as the inner boundary of a containing body, like the inner boundary of a ball which contains air inside. But place is a continuous quantity not because of its whole definition—for the fact that the container has a body inside it is not investigated by geometry—but because of a part of that definition, namely, 'surface'; so place is or has a surface, and all the properties of

surfaces are investigated by the geometer.

Place as an inner boundary is a surface, and the parts of place, which would have to be parts of that surface, are themselves surfaces. From the text it is not clear whether Aristotle here regards place as an inner boundary or as the space inside that boundary. The word 'occupy' suggests the space; and by the word 'body' in the phrase 'which the parts of the body occupy' he seems to mean the contained body. But some of the parts of the contained body do not touch the place as defined in the *Physics*, i.e., as the inner boundary of the containing body, and so the boundaries of those parts would not be parts of the inner boundary of the containing body. This is another indication that the *Categories* was written before the *Physics*.

9. A line is one thing and is continuous. As continuous, it has parts which must be lines and not points (231a21-b6), and each such part must be joined or have a point in common with some other part. Hence each part has a position relative to the other parts and to the whole line. The same applies to surfaces and solids.

Why refer the line to a plane? But lines cannot exist apart from planes or surfaces, for they are related to these by being present in them. Hence the position of a part of a line may be related either to another part, or to the whole line itself, or to the plane or surface (or even the body) in which the line is present.

10. The parts of 10 as a mere number, for example, have no order among themselves, just as they have no position and no contact; but it is in counting the parts to arrive at that number that we attribute an order to those parts as the number of the parts counted increases. It makes no difference which of the ten units we take as first, which second, etc., yet there is an order, not in the parts as parts of the number itself, but in our counting, for we say 'one, two, etc.' up to the last unit. Perhaps it is because of this fact that Aristotle adds the phrase 'and in this way there might be an order'.

11. In other words, in saying that the white is much, we mean that its surface is much and not its whiteness *as such*; for the thing (whether the body or its white surface) which is called 'white' is much in virtue of its surface and not its whiteness, but it is called 'white' because whiteness is present in it or in its surface also, whether as an accident or always. Speaking directly or in the fundamental sense, then, we say 'the surface is much', but indirectly (i.e., through some other attribute possessed by the surface or the thing with that surface) we say 'the white is much'. Thus the white (or whiteness) *as such* is not a quantity and has no attribute of a quantity; but if we are to speak of it as having such an attribute, this is because that attribute belongs to a quantity which exists along with the whiteness in the thing which is white.

12. From 6a19-22, 15b19-21, and 856b2-5 it is evident that the word δίπηχυ signifies a magnitude and not a number, and for this *reason* we

translate it as 'a line two cubits long', in which 'two cubits long' merely quantifies numerically the line, and a line is a magnitude. The appearance of numerical measurement in that expression is just a device to let us know how long that line is as a magnitude, so 'two cubits long' is given as a descriptive predicate of a line, which is a magnitude.

13. The argument in lines 5b26-9 appears to be the same as the preceding, but it is not. The preceding argument starts with a thing rather than the corresponding name and states that when the thing is called 'great', it is referred to some other thing. This argument starts with the name 'great' rather than the thing itself and states that it is a relative name, having 'small' for its correlative, and that each of these names is relative because it signifies a reference to something else when predicated of a thing.

14. If, according to 6a36-8b24, things which are somehow referred to something else are said to be relatives, then Aristotle seems to be saying here that relatives cannot be contraries. But virtue and vice, which are relatives as genera, are stated as being contraries in 6b15-7; and likewise for *knowledge* and ignorance. We shall discuss this point when we come to 6b15.

15. Argument (a) goes as follows. The hypothesis is made that the great and the small are contraries; and the upholder of this hypothesis may assert that the same thing can be called both 'great' and 'small' at the same time, giving as an example the fact that a thing is great relative to A but small relative to B. This example, of course, is sophistic, because the thing is great and small at the same time but not in the same respect, for 'relative to A' and 'relative to B' signify different respects; and any other example he might choose would be likewise sophistic. Anyway, since contraries cannot belong to a thing at the same time, the great and the small cannot be contraries.

16. Argument (b), though not spelled out, may be viewed as follows. If the great and small are, *as such*, quantities and not relations, then a quantity which is called 'small' and also 'great' is so named by its nature and not by any of its relations or its attributes. So if 'great' and 'small' signify the nature or part of the nature of one and the same quantity, that quantity would be contrary to itself; for what we call 'great' and 'small' would be one and the same thing, and the great is assumed to be contrary to the small. Hence if we are to admit that the same thing is both great and small, we have to reject the assumption that the great and the small are contraries.

17. The expressions 'up' and 'down' come under the category 'somewhere' and do not signify quantities; so even if they are posited as contraries, they are no evidence that quantities can be contrary to each other.

The definition of contraries in terms of greatest distance, of course, is too limited and would imply that qualities and many other things would not be contraries or would not admit of contraries. Whiteness is most different from blackness but it is not at any distance from it, except metaphorically; and if the distance between evenness and oddness were the greatest, then 20 would be further from 19 than from 4, for 20 and 4 are both even, but 19 is odd.

18. Are the names 'equality', 'inequality', 'greater', 'less', and others like them univocal? If not, then is the name 'quantity' univocal and hence a single category or not?

If 'equality' were univocal, any quantity would be either equal or unequal to any other. But this is not the case, for though one line is equal or unequal to another line, it is neither equal nor unequal to a surface or a solid or time or place; for a solid is not made out of surfaces, nor a surface out of lines, nor a line out of points, and comparison of one kind of quantity with another kind with respect to equality and inequality is impossible (215b18-9, 231a21-9, 1001b18-9, 1077a34-5). Further, an axiom such as 'if equals are added to equals, the sums are equal' is true of all quantities not univocally but by analogy (76a37-b2); hence it must be qualified, i.e., the quantities to be added must be of the same kind if their sums are to be equal or unequal. If so, then such an axiom is like the principle of contradiction (1005b11-34) and the other axioms of all beings (or of all things); for 'being' or 'thing' is not univocal but analogical and has many allied senses (1028a10-31), and it is not a genus with the categories as species (92b14, 998b22-7). So if the name 'quantity' is like the name 'being', it would appear that the kinds of things which are called 'quantities' but are not comparable with respect to equality and inequality are categories, even if these kinds have a closer relation to each other than to the other categories (for lines are in surfaces, surfaces are in solids, etc., but no such close relation appears to exist among the other categories). Perhaps similar arguments apply to what are called 'qualities'.

7

1. In Greek two words are used for 'relative' or 'relation', πρός τι, which may be literally translated as 'relative to something', or 'in relation to something', or 'with reference to something'; but linguistically they seem to be used sometimes as a noun and sometimes as an adjective, like 'white' and 'good'.

2. For the Greek word ὅπερ we use the expression *as such*. The word is frequently used as a technical word by Aristotle without being explained or defined in the extant works, and this fact calls for an interpretation.

If the thing before us is the number ten, we may call it 'ten', or 'a number', or 'double', or 'double of five', or 'greater than six', or in many other ways. Now to be ten, to be a number, to be double, and to be greater than six are all different in their nature or essence, but the subject which underlies all of them here is ten, for each of them is either said of ten or is · present in ten. If one asks what is the double of five, the answer by way of definition, which signifies the nature of a thing, may be either the definition of ten or the definition of the double of five. But the two definitions differ, for the first signifies analytically the nature of the subject ten but the second signifies analytically the nature of something present in ten, namely, the relation of being double of five. By saying 'if, *as such*, they are said to be . . .' Aristotle appears to mean that the nature or part of the nature of a relative—and relatives are always present in things which are not relatives, perhaps with some exceptions, such as *knowledge* in relation to mathematics—is such that it must include a reference to something other than the thing in which it is present. Thus, to call ten 'double' would not be enough, for a reference to something else is needed; but to call it 'double of five' might be sufficient. The expression 'double of five', then, signifies *as such* (i.e., insofar as it is a relative, or in virtue of its nature) not ten but a reference to something else, to five, although the subject of that relation is ten. Another way of saying this is that a relative as a relative, or insofar as it is a relative, or in virtue of its nature as a relative, must have or include a reference to something other than the subject in which it is present.

A problem still remains: how does 'double of five' differ from 'double of a half'; and does each of them signify a relative? The first is limited as a predicate to ten; the second has universal applicability. Perhaps 'double of five' has 'half of ten' as its correlative, whereas 'double of a half' has 'half of a double' as its correlative.

The expression '*as such*' is not limited to relatives but has universal application. Thus if A *as such* is B, then B is either the nature of A or a part of that nature; e.g., Socrates *as such* is a man, or rational, or a substance, but not wise or brave or Greek or healthy, for none of the latter is a part of his nature, which is, let us say, a rational animal and nothing more.

3. Usually, names signifying relatives in the English language are followed by such words as 'of', 'by', 'to', 'than', and the like, as in 'master of a slave', 'known by knowledge', 'greater than five', and so on, and perhaps in Greek the genitive (indicated in English by 'of') is most frequently used; but this convention varies from language to language. In English we use 'greater than' but in Greek usually the genitive is used after what is translated as 'greater'.

We must distinguish the expression λέγεται τινός, which we translate as 'said to be of' in connection with relatives, from λέγεται κατὰ τινός, which we translate as 'said of' in Section 2.

4. One may raise the problem as to whether these are relatives or not, and the same applies to virtue and vice in line 6b16, for some of them are

listed under the category of quality also (11a20-38). Perhaps the meaning of 'relation' has not yet been fully determined.

5. One might say that possession is of the possessed, *knowledge* is of the *known*, sensation is of the sensible, and likewise with the others.

6. To use an analogy, 'bravery' is to 'brave' as 'standing' is to 'to stand'; and just as 'brave' is a derivative name, so is 'to stand'. Instances of 'to stand' are 'stands' as in 'he stands' and 'stood' as in 'she stood'.

7. The word 'ignorance' has two meanings; for it means (a) absence of any *thought*, and (b) mistaken *thought* (79b23-8). Ignorance as the contrary of *knowledge* is ignorance in sense (b), but ignorance in sense (a) is the contradictory of *knowledge*. The correlative of *knowledge* is the *known*, for *knowledge* is of the *known*; and in the case of ignorance in sense (b), perhaps no name exists, or else it is the *misknown* (or the mistakenly *known*, if you wish). Virtue as a relative will be considered in Comm. 21 of Section 8, but it is evident that its contrary is vice.

We may now return to the apparent contradiction indicated in Commentary 14 of the preceding Section. The great and the small (or better, the greater and the smaller) are correlatives, and Aristotle says that correlatives are not contraries. But *knowledge* and ignorance are not correlatives, for neither is *knowledge* said to be the *knowledge* of (or by or etc.) ignorance, nor is ignorance said to be the ignorance of (or by, or etc.) *knowledge*. The same applies to virtue and vice which, as genera, are regarded as relatives.

8. Evidently, 6 is more unequal to 20 than 19 is; but it is not evident that equality admits of degree, for 6 is unequal to 20, and so is 19, and the only number which is equal to 20 is 20, or (16 + 4) if you wish, and this equality does not admit a variation of degree. If it is said that 19 is more equal to 20 than 6 is, in view of the smaller difference between 19 and 20, one may likewise say that 9 is more a double of 4 than 24 is, for 9 is close to being a double of 4 but 24 is not so close. But it is stated that the double does not admit of variation of degree but that the equal does.

9. If A is relative to B and B is a relative, we may call B 'the correlative of A'; and we shall call the pair A and B 'correlatives'. So since correlatives have reciprocal reference to each other, either A or B may be the correlative of the other.

The Greek for 'of the sensible' is $\alpha\dot{\iota}\sigma\theta\eta\tau o\hat{v}$, whose case is genitive; but the Greek for 'by sensation' is $\alpha\dot{\iota}\sigma\theta\dot{\eta}\sigma\epsilon\iota$, and its case is dative.

10. Insects and bats, too, have wings. The expression 'the wing of a bird' is like the expression 'knowledge of Peter'; and just as Peter is a substance and not a relative, so a bird is a substance and not a relative. But neither do we say that Peter is Peter of (or by or etc.) knowledge, nor do we say that a bird is the bird of (or by or etc.) the wing. The fact that a given wing belongs to a bird does not make both the wing and the bird correlatives.

11. If what is stated up to here, in this sentence, is to be true, then slaves and masters need not be men; in fact, there are leaders and followers among other animals also.

12. Perhaps he has in mind the practical or the productive arts, which are included under '*knowledge*' taken in a wide sense. 1065a4-5.

13. By definition, *knowledge* is of that which exists, in fact, mainly of that which exists necessarily or eternally (1139b18-24); and that which so exists cannot fail to exist. If so, the phrase 'when the *known* is negated' is an assumption which, at least for that which is eternal, cannot become true; but one may make this assumption as a hypothesis for the sake of argument, whether the assumption can be true of anything or not. Thus to show that 2 is prior in existence to 5 one can argue thus: 'If 5 exists, 2 must exist, but if 2 exists, it is not necessary for 5 to exist', even if as a matter of fact 5 always or necessarily exists. 14a29-35.

14. Evidently, at Aristotle's time the problem of squaring the circle, whether by ruler and compass or in some other way, was not yet proved to be possible or impossible.

15. An objection may be raised. If animals are negated, men or *knowers*, too, will be negated (unless one includes God as a *knower*, and one may rule this out, in view of the kind of God's activity as indicated in Book Lambda, *Metaphysics*); and since only man begets man (1070a28), if men do not exist, there will never be any *knowers*. Then existing things, too, will never be *knowable*.

16. The objection in the previous Commentary might be repeated here, but it is somewhat weak; for if all animals are negated, some of them might be generated by chance (898b4-11). In either case, however, if the expression 'sensation of an object' means the actual sensing of that object, then perhaps the correlative of such sensation should be the sensed object while it is being sensed, and not before or after; and in that case a sensation and what is being sensed will exist simultaneously. But if 'sensation' means the faculty of sensing and the correlative of that sensation is the sensible, with the usual meaning of the word 'sensible', simultaneity is not necessary. The word αἰσθητόν (= 'sensible') means that which can be sensed and also that which is being sensed; and αἴσθησις means actual sensing and also the power of sensation. These distinctions are not made here but elsewhere. 417a9-14, 426a15-27.

17. The word 'of' in 'A of B' has many senses in English, and likewise in Greek, but the sense intended here is that in which A is a primary substance which *as such* is posited as being relative to another primary substance. The expression 'Socrates of X', where X is the father of Socrates, is an abbreviation of 'Socrates, the son of X', and so the word 'of' in it does not have the meaning intended by Aristotle. So if the word 'of' is used to indicate a reference to a correlative, then 'Socrates of X' would be a

meaningless expression.

18. Whereas a father is always a father of a child, a man is not or cannot be a man of anything; and 'a man of honor' is an idiomatic way of saying 'an honorable man'.

19. One may raise an objection; for a relation (or a relative) is a category and so an ultimate genus, and an ultimate genus cannot have a definition. Perhaps 'property' or 'description' would be a better word, like the property of quantity given in the *Metaphysics* in 1020a7-8. Is Aristotle using ὁρισμός (= 'definition') in a different sense here? 1014b9-10.

20. Another expression for 'whose being' is 'whose essence' or 'whose nature'. Accordingly, a relative as now defined must have reference to some other thing, for its nature is to be such; but if one says 'A is said to be of B', it does not follow that A cannot be understood by itself without B. Thus 'A is said to be of B' as a definition of a relative is wider than the one now given. To understand definitely a relative as now defined, then, one must definitely understand something else also, but to understand definitely A in 'A is said to be of B' one may sometimes be able to definitely understand A without B. The reciprocal reference of a relative to its correlative, stated in 6b28-7b14, is not mentioned here, but it follows, whether as a property or an attribute or belonging to correlatives in some other way, from the revised definition.

21. Since 'being' and 'the essence of' or 'the nature of' have the same meaning, to state what it is to be a relative one must give neither more nor less than the definition of a relative; for a definition is a statement of the essence or nature of a thing. 1015a11-3, 1031a12-4.

22. An alternative to 'wholly' is 'at all', but the two expressions differ in meaning; for if one does not understand something wholly, he may still understand it partly. Which expression is the correct translation? According to the first example which follows, it seems that to understand definitely that 10 is a double one must understand also that it is the double of 5, which is definite, otherwise his understanding will be partial or incomplete or, as stated in the second example, inaccurate or an assumption and not *knowledge*. So perhaps 'wholly' is correct; and 'to understand wholly' and 'to understand definitely' either imply each other or are the same or close in meaning, or else 'wholly' applies to 'double of 5' but 'definitely' applies to '5'.

23. An expression such as 'greater than 3' appears to give rise to some difficulties. If to understand a relative, *as such*, one must understand its correlative also, as in the case of the greater and the less, and if to understand a relative, *as such*, in a definite way one must understand in a definite way its correlative also, then though 'greater than 3' appears to signify something definite, it may signify 4 or 5 or some other number.

Perhaps 'greater than 3' does not signify something definite but should have as its correlative the expression 'less than 4', and both these are in a certain sense indefinite expressions, though they are more definite than 'greater' and 'less'. By 'greater than 3' we mean a (whole) number which is greater than 3. But 'greater than 3 by 2' signifies something definite, and this is 5; and its correlative would then be 'less than 5 by 2', and this signifies something definite, which is 3. So to understand 5 and 3 not as numbers or as members of two sets of numbers but as correlatives, we should understand 5 as greater than 3 by 2, and 3 as less than 5 by 2. This is analogous to understanding John as the master of Peter and Peter as the slave of John, if these are related as master and slave, respectively.

24. According to 1017b10-3 and 1028b9-10, parts of bodies, too, are said to be substances. But a part which has a function must be related *as such* to the whole of which it is a part and must be defined in terms of the whole (1035b4-25); and if so, then *knowledge* of a hand or a head must include *knowledge* of an animal. But *knowledge* of an animal does not include *knowledge* of a hand or a head, so there is no reciprocal reference. On the other hand, one cannot definitely *know* that X is a slave if he does not *know* definitely whose slave X is, for to call X 'a slave' may be an assumption; but one can definitely *know* an individual hand as being a hand by observing it functioning even if the rest of the man's body is concealed, for he would *know* that it is a hand of a man, even if he does not *know* who that man is.

There is also the problem of whether a part comes under any category or not. For a part exists potentially and not actually, and *as such* it is not one, or else it is one potentially.

Perhaps Aristotle was not sure of his position, as is evident from the last sentence of this Section.

8

1. In the list of categories given in 1b25-7 the neuter noun ποιόν is translated as 'quality', but this word may be translated as 'qualitative' or as 'qualitative thing' also. Here, the noun ποιότης is used, and its translation can be only 'quality'.

2. The word τινές is masculine in gender, and it appears to refer to men; and the tendency is to translate it as 'people' or as 'some men'. But from what follows concerning qualities, it appears that they are present in all kinds of things. So we translate the word as 'some things'. Perhaps Aristotle is using τινές to include all genders, for there seems to be no name in Greek to perform this function.

3. Literally, the Greek name for 'such and such' is derived from the Greek name for 'quality' and has the form of an adjective. So an alternative

to 'such and such' would be 'qualitative'. We shall continue to use 'such and such' most of the time.

4. The name 'science' here signifies not a relation but a quality, i.e., that which one has acquired after a study, like mathematics. As a name for a relative, 'science' is a genus whose correlative is 'scientifically known', as in the case of 'knowledge' and 'known'; but as a name signifying a quality, it is a sort of species of that genus, and an example of such a name would be 'science of quantities' or 'mathematics', which signifies a quality possessed by a mathematician. The same applies to 'virtue'; and virtues as qualities would be bravery, temperance, and the like.

5. Whether 'chill' signifies the condition of the body, or the feeling which accompanies the condition, or any of the two, is not clear; and likewise for 'hotness' or 'hot condition'. In either case, hotness and chills do not last long, and so they are dispositions and not habits.

6. The contradiction is only apparent. In the absence of a Greek name, Aristotle often uses the same name in two senses, as a genus and as one species of that genus. The name 'disposition' as a genus, then, has as its species 'habit' and 'disposition' in the limited sense as stated in 8b26-8. Other names which Aristotle uses like 'disposition' are 'chance' and 'substance', and to distinguish the two senses for each such name we usually use italics for the species or limited sense but not for the genus; e.g., in the *Physics* we use *'chance'* for the species but 'chance' for the genus. 197a36b1.

7. Evidently, 'healthy' has two meanings, and it is the adjective derived from 'health' and 'healthiness'. Health is the disposition of a healthy person when he is not sick, and it is the kind of quality indicated in 8b35-9a1; but healthiness is a natural capability which tends to keep a man healthy, and this capability is possessed by that man even when he happens to be sick for some strong reason.

8. According to Ackrill, Aristotle's discussion of capabilities is not thorough or complete, for he says that Aristotle leaves out (a) general capabilities of doing or suffering something, such as the mere capability of learning trigonometry or of breaking, whether with ease or difficulty, (b) acquired capabilities, (c) abilities to acquire or retain capabilities to do or suffer something, and (d) others.

Acquired capabilities are not left out, for these are the qualities which are called 'habits' and 'dispositions'. As for general capabilities, they belong to the nature of things and would be indicated by the forms or the differentiae of things. Vision, for example, is a part of the soul, which is the form of an animal. The ability to learn trigonometry follows from the ability to learn rational things and the fact that trigonometry is rational. The capability of not being easily broken is in the nature of a diamond and other such bodies. Such capabilities are properties of things or are indicated by the differentiae of things, and differentiae are one kind of qualities (1020a33-b1), not qualities without qualification, like the white, but analogous to those indicated in 3b10-23. As for capabilities of type (c), these would follow from or come under (a), for such is the ability to learn an art, by means of which one creates a work of art. Finally, Aristotle admits the possibility of having omitted some qualities; but none of those considered by Ackrill as capabilities appear to have been excluded.

9. These complexions, though caused by external agents, may still be called 'affective qualities' insofar as they produce on others an affection with respect to sensation. But they are not like the qualities of snow or fire, for fire is always hot and heats by its nature, and snow is always white and produces cold by its nature, whereas men are not always pale or always tan nor are they pale or tan by their nature, but only when affected. What about the blackness of black men? Is it like the whiteness of snow?

10. Perhaps 'affective qualities' would be the accurate expression, for in 9a28-9 affections have already been stated to be one kind of qualities.

11. The term 'blusher' signifies a man who has the habit of blushing and not just the affection, for an affection need not arise from habit, and so he who blushes need not be a blusher; and the same applies to 'pale man' as used here.

12. A triangle is a quantity, and 'such and such' refers to its differentia, which is three-sidedness. Similarly, when a line is called 'straight', it is called so in virtue of its straightness. The name 'curvature' here must be taken to signify a quality and not a number. Curvature as a number is something different; it is the measurement corresponding to curvature as a quality, like the number of vibrations per second of a sound corresponding to the sensation of that sound. Perhaps it should be called 'number of curvature'.

13. One may raise some difficulties. The sensation caused by a smooth surface is different from that caused by a rough surface, and such sensations are qualities or affections caused by things which are in some way similar as causes to whiteness, for whiteness causes the sensation of whiteness. Should we not, then, regard roughness and smoothness as qualities, or else regard them as we do straightness and curvature? Perhaps things which cause qualities need not be qualities. Again, shape and *form*, if taken as qualities, seem to be differentiae of geometrical objects, which are quantities. Analogous differentiae might be mentioned of numbers, such as oddness, evenness, and the like, and differentiae in other categories might be included also. In fact, differentiae in all categories, including substance, are mentioned in the *Metaphysics* (1020a33-b1) as forming one kind of qualities, and this fact seems to suggest that the *Categories* is an earlier work. It appears, then, that what Aristotle calls 'qualities' are not as close to each other in their nature as the two kinds of quantities, and one may even

wonder whether 'quality' is univocally predicable of all of them.

14. In Greek there was a single word for 'a natural runner', and likewise for 'a natural boxer'; and no single word existed for each of the corresponding qualities, but phrases were used to signify them. To distinguish derivatively the natural ability to box from that which is acquired scientifically, we use the two expressions 'a natural boxer' and 'a boxer', but in Greek one word, πυκτικός, was used for both. So a natural boxer is one who inherited the capability to become an effective boxer with ease, but a boxer is one who learned the rules of boxing and uses them to the best of his ability.

15. We are using the words 'integrity' and 'upright' instead of 'virtue' and 'virtuous', respectively, because in English 'virtuous' is derived from 'virtue' but in Greek the word for 'virtuous' is not derived from the name for 'virtue'.

16. By 'named with respect to' he means derivatively named, as in the case of 'virtuous' from virtue, or else, named in some other way, as in the case of 'upright' from integrity.

17. From what follows, it is evident that things named *by* a quality are posited as being either qualities or things with qualities. The latter are derivatively named from qualities, like the just and the brave, or named in some other way, like the upright from integrity. Evidently, Aristotle uses ποιόν in two senses, as stated in Comm. 2 of Section 4, and here ποιόν includes both senses and is translated as 'things named by a quality'. See also next Commentary.

18. From what follows, that which, being one and the same in nature, admits a variation of degree is not the quality itself but the substance or subject which has that quality and is derivatively named from that quality, and it may vary with respect to that quality. Only substances can change; qualities and all the others cannot change. 224b11-3.

19. Just as only quantities can be equal or unequal to each other, so only with respect to quality may things be like or unlike each other. The senses of 'like' and 'unlike' are given in 1018a15-9. The difficulties we raised in Comm. 18 of Section 6 concerning quantity as being one genus may be repeated here, and even more so; for the kinds of quantities do not appear to be as many as the kinds of qualities, and there seems to be less accuracy and less unity in qualities than in quantities. Moreover, there is a universal science whose objects are all quantities in general, even if they are treated in an analogous manner (74a4-25, 76a37-b2, 1026a25-7, 1064b8-9), but there is doubt whether a universal science is possible for all qualities in general.

20. If one calls grammar 'a science' without specifying it further, then he calls it by a name which signifies a relation. In expressions such as 'the grammar of science', of course, the name 'grammar' is used metaphorically,

or else, in another sense; for, if grammar be defined as the science of the correct usage of words, then 'the grammar of science' would be 'the science of the correct usage of words of science', and the latter expression is meaningless or else useless as a discipline.

21. As a genus, *knowledge* is of the *known* and the *known* is *known* by *knowledge*, and these two are posited as correlatives. Similarly, a possession (or a habit) as a genus is of the possessed, and the possessed is possessed by possession. In the case of virtue as a genus, it is a relative in a similar way, but no name exists for its correlative, although we may say that virtue is of the virtuous or of that of which it is a virtue; but 'virtuous' in this case is not used as a derivative name but must signify *as such* something related to virtue, like the *known* as related to *knowledge*, for the *known as such* is *known* by *knowledge*, and the virtuous *as such* is virtuous by being similarly referred to virtue. And just as that which underlies the *known* is a thing (for '*known*' is predicable of that thing), so that which underlies the virtuous is, let us say, a certain kind of *action* but not the man who performs that *action* (for 'virtuous' as applied to that man is a derivative name and has a different meaning).

As a species, *knowledge* is specified by including its object, and so it has no need to be referred to something else as to a correlative; but as specified *knowledge*, it is present in something, in the soul, and *as such* it is a quality. For example, such is the *knowledge* a man has when he can demonstrate that the medians of a triangle are concurrent, or that the sum $1 + 3 + 5 + \ldots + (2n-1)$ is a square integer, namely, n^2. In the same way, a specific virtue would be, for example, justice or temperance or bravery, and *as such* it is a quality. Similar remarks apply to a disposition as a genus and as a species, and to all others like it.

22. Lines 11a20-38 do not seem to be consistent with Aristotle's position elsewhere. How can a univocal name come under two categories if these are assumed to be mutually exclusive? For if a relative *as such* must have reference to something else, so should some qualities according to lines 11a20-38; but nothing is said about this in the discussion of quality. Lines 120b36-1a9 and 145a13-8 state that the differentia and hence the species of a relative is a relative and that a genus and its species must be in the same category, and no exception is mentioned. Thus science as a genus is subdivided into theoretical, practical, and productive, and the multiple is subdivided into the double, the triple, etc. Again, one function of a differentia is to specify further some things which come under a given genus (1058a6-8), not to change the category by way of that differentia.

Another difficulty arises in connection with *knowledge* and particular *knowledge*. Mathematics as particular *knowledge* is posited as a quality, but *knowledge* is posited as a relative; yet just as *knowledge* is referred to the *known*, so mathematical *knowledge* may be referred to the mathematically *known*. The same may be said of virtue and the others. If virtue as a genus is of the virtuous as a genus, a particular virtue may be of the particular virtuous. Moreover, if virtue as a genus is defined in terms of a certain *action*, a right *action*, justice, too, may be defined in terms of a certain kind of *action* towards others.

Perhaps there is some reason in positing '*knowledge*' and '*knowledge* of something' under different categories, for the former appears to be incomplete in some sense while the latter does not; and in view of this, perhaps the former is regarded as a relative while the latter is regarded as a quality. Under '*knowledge* of something', then, we would have, for example, *knowledge* of things as things, *knowledge* of quantities as quantities, *knowledge* of magnitudes as magnitudes, etc., and these qualities go by the names of 'metaphysics', 'mathematics', 'geometry', etc., respectively. Under '*knowledge*', on the other hand, we would have metaphysical *knowledge*, mathematical *knowledge*, geometrical *knowledge*, etc., respectively; and these would be relatives. Evidently, mathematical *knowledge* is different from mathematics (or *knowledge* of quantities), and similarly for the others; for mathematical *knowledge* is a relative and is of the mathematically *known*, but mathematics is a quality. As for '*knowledge* of mathematics', literally it signifies neither mathematics nor mathematical *knowledge* but something else, perhaps knowledge of the definition of mathematics, for *knowledge* of a thing is knowledge of its causes (71b9-12), and the causes of mathematics as a quality would be stated in the definition of mathematics.

If the above distinctions are granted, then the manner in which science is the genus of theoretical science is different from that in which science is the genus of mathematics. In the first case, science as a relation remains a relation when further specified, for theoretical science is of the theoretically known. In the second, science changes to a quality by a specification of that of which it is the science, for mathematics is not the mathematics of anything. Accordingly, it appears that science may be a genus in two different ways. Is this possible, or is the word 'genus' used in two different senses? See Comm. 5 of Section 11.

Finally, since ποιόν as a noun is translated as 'quality', but as an adjective it is translated as 'qualitative' or 'such and such', and similarly for the name πρός τι, perhaps an alternative translation of lines 11a37-8 would be: 'Moreover, if the same thing should happen to be both relative to something and qualitative [i.e., such and such], there would be nothing absurd in listing it under both genera'. If so, the thing would be listed under the two genera not as a subject, whatever this may be, but in virtue of (a) being relative to one thing and (b) having a quality. For example, the same man may be called 'father' and 'temperate', which are derivative names; and fatherhood is a relation whereas temperance is a quality. If this translation and the interpretation given are correct, the difficulties indicated seem to disappear.

9

1. A difficulty arises with respect to some of the categories other than those already discussed, for it appears that acting, being acted upon, and some of the others are relatives. If to be a relative is to be somehow referred to something else (8a31-2), and if to understand a relative in a definite way is to understand in a definite way that to which it is referred (8a35-7), then it appears that acting is a relative, and the same applies to being acted upon; for that which acts does so on something else, and acting is referred to that which is being acted upon, and to understand in a definite way that which acts *as such*, i.e., as acting, one will have to understand in a definite way that on which it acts, otherwise acting would be an assumption, as suggested in 8b10-1. Further, Aristotle lists 'that which can act' and 'that which can be acted upon' as expressions signifying relatives in the *Metaphysics* (1020b26-30); and it would seem that to act is more likely to be a relative than to be able to act, for the latter requires only the ability, which is a quality, whereas the former requires also something to act upon.

There seems to be another difficulty. Bravery is a quality, and the name 'brave', which is derived from 'bravery', signifies a subject with bravery and not a thing under a new category. But κεῖσθαι (= 'being in a position'), which is stated in 6b11-4 and in 11b8-10 to be a name derived from θέσις (= 'position'), is put forward as a category and not as signifying a subject in a position; and position comes under relation.

10

1. Opposites are discussed also in 1018a20-b8, 1022b22-3a7, and 1054a20-9a14, and they are made use of in 113b15-4a25 and 135b7-6a13. Since opposites exist in all categories, the general discussion of opposites appears to belong to *Metaphysics*, and the same may be said of priority, simultaneity, motion, and the various senses of 'having'; and all are discussed in the *Metaphysics*, except motion, which is discussed in the *Physics*. One may raise the question, then, whether the part from here to the end was originally a part of the *Categories* or was put here by an editor.

2. The pair 'good' and 'bad' as contrary names may be taken generically, but if a particular pair is given, there should be a reference to the same genus or subject. For example, the contrary of health should be disease and no other thing which is bad, and what is the same here is the

genus of health and sickness, which we may call 'the bodily disposition of an animal'.

3. We may state the difference by way of example as follows. As an example of correlatives we may take the double and the half, and each of these must be referred, *as such*, to the other. As an example of contraries we may take the good and the bad, but each of these is not referred, *as such*, to the other. Of course, by calling the good 'the contrary of the bad' we seem to relate it to the bad, but the good *as such* is neither understood nor defined in terms of the bad and need not be related to the bad. In fact, we may relate any two things, if we wish, however apart they happen to be in their nature; for we may say that a triangle is related to a square by being different from it, and that a color is distinct from a number, and 'difference' and 'distinction' are relative names. But such relations are infinite and are not a part of the nature of the thing, otherwise *knowledge* of the nature of anything would be impossible, for we cannot traverse the infinite. Indeed, even partial *knowledge* of a thing's nature would be impossible, for to *know* a part of the thing's nature we would still have to traverse the infinite.

But, one may ask, is it not possible in some cases for one contrary to be referred, *as such*, to its contrary, whether by way of definition or of understanding? Oddness and evenness are contraries in numbers, and evenness may be defined as divisibility of a number into two equal numbers while oddness may be defined as indivisibility of a number into two equal numbers; and the indivisible appears to be defined in terms of the divisible. Or better, divisibility and indivisibility are opposed as contraries, and the definition of indivisibility appears to include divisibility, which is prior to indivisibility because of sensation (1054a20-9). The objection to this argument may be that priority in *knowledge* is not priority in sensation, but that what is prior in *knowledge* is usually posterior in sensation (1018b30-4). Still, since being is prior to nonbeing and nonbeing is known through being or is defined through being (86b34-6)—e.g., not-man is known or defined through man—it appears that, in some cases at least, one of two contraries is known or defined through the other (1129a17-21).

Perhaps more distinctions are needed to settle the difficulty. The meanings of 'contrary' and 'privation' as used here, we may add, are not altogether the same as those given in the *Metaphysics*. 1018a20-38, 1022b22-3a7, 1054a20-5b29.

4. The Greek word ὑπάρχειν, translated as 'to belong' and first introduced here, seems wider in its application than 'to be present in' or 'to be said of' or 'to be predicable of' or perhaps all of them combined; and it is used exclusively after 12b29 till the end of the *Categories*. For example, Aristotle would say that the equality of the angles of a triangle to two right angles belongs to a triangle, and that Socrates belongs to the speaker in 'the speaker is Socrates'; but perhaps 'belongs' in these cases is not used in any

of the senses of the three expressions above. The name is also used in the treatise *On Propositions*, in *Prior* and *Posterior Analytics*, and elsewhere. 24a16-22, 25a1-13, 29b29-35, 48a40-b9, 49a6-10.

5. The names 'virtuous' and 'vicious' in the narrow sense are predicable only of men, whether directly or indirectly; for if predicable of things belonging to men, such as their virtuous and vicious ethical habits and *actions*, they are indirectly predicable of men, since *actions*, too, belong only to men. The two names are used in a wider sense also; but it is not clear whether Aristotle is using them here in the narrow or in the wide sense, for the subjects of which they are predicable in a wide sense may be actions of other animals, or things belonging to the body, such as health, strength, and beauty, or even inanimate objects, such as a violin. 1106a19-21, 1360b21-2.

6. Virtue and vice in a man are habits, and these take time to develop. Hence a baby, though capable of virtue or vice when it grows up, is not yet virtuous or vicious. The word 'man', we may add, is predicable of a baby.

7. Instances of 'to be blind' are 'is blind', 'am blind', and 'are blind', and these appear to be derivative names, for they are predicable of substances. But 'blindness' is not predicable of a substance, for it is not a derivative name. We are using 'being blind' and 'to be blind' synonymously, and similarly for 'having vision' and 'to have vision'.

8. Since an affirmation and its denial cannot both be true at the same time (for one of them must be true and the other false when the subject is universally taken or is an individual, 17b26-37), the objects signified by them cannot be facts at the same time; but if both objects are facts, then they are signified at different times. Now in the opposition of a possession and the corresponding privation there is no reference to time; but since an affirmation and its denial signify also time, a problem arises. If the time signified is the same, the opposition of what is signified is between a being and the corresponding nonbeing, e.g., between an actual sitting Socrates and the nonexistence of this; but if the signified objects are facts, the opposition will be between facts signified at different times, e.g., between Socrates when sitting and Socrates when not sitting. At different times, of course, the objects signified need not be both facts, but in such cases perhaps the corresponding oppositions, if they are to be called 'oppositions' at all, should be qualified or excluded. The text seems to favor the opposition between facts, for Aristotle uses the word πρᾶγμα for the objects which are signified, and this word appears to signify an actual being or fact; but lines 13a37-b3 seem to favor the other alternative.

9. Although the name 'vision' is present in the definition of blindness, blindness is not of vision or by vision or referred to vision in any of the ways in which correlatives are referred to each other, for a privation is a kind of

negation (1055b3-4), and a negation is not regarded as an instance of a reference.

10. The statement 'men are white' is an affirmation and 'men are not white' is its denial, but they are both true according to 17b26-33 and 18a8-12; for the subject, though universal, is not universally taken; and similarly for other pairs such as this. It appears, then, that Aristotle is not including or is not aware of such pairs of statements here, and this may be another indication that the *Categories*, or this part of it at least, was written before the main works and the work *On Propositions*.

11. Whether these opposites are things or the names signifying those things makes no difference, for in either case they are not composites; and even if some of them can be expressed as composites (e.g., instead of 'oddness' one may use 'indivisibility of a number into two equal parts'), still no time element enters into those composites, and such element is necessary if an expression is to be true or false in the fundamental sense. 17a9-12.

12. The literal translation should be 'Socrates's being healthy' and 'Socrates's being sick', and these seem to refer to the objects or facts and not to the corresponding statements; but the next sentence mentions truth or falsity as an attribute, and this seems to imply that the reference is to the statements and not to the objects or to the facts signified by those statements. The same occurs later in lines 13b22-33. But 'truth' is sometimes used as a predicate of a fact, for it has two senses. Anyway, whether statements or what they signify, they are not the type of contraries already considered, for Aristotle is discussing primary contraries and not composites which have contraries as parts. Healthy Socrates and sick Socrates are contrary in virtue of health and sickness, respectively, which are primary contraries, but not in virtue of Socrates, who underlies health and sickness and is the same, whether in health or disease; for Socrates is not contrary to himself. The word 'contrary', of course, has other allied meanings also, and contraries which are statements are considered in the treatise *On Propositions*. Contraries are discussed comprehensively in the *Metaphysics*, 1018a25-35 and 1055a3-b29.

13. The remarks in the preceding Commentary apply here also.

14. A better example would be 'Socrates is toothless' and 'Socrates has teeth', when Socrates is a week old; for 'toothless' is the contrary and not the contradictory of 'having teeth' and so it is not a synonym of 'having no teeth'. Accordingly, both statements will be false.

15. For Aristotle, another way of stating the meaning of 'Socrates is not sick' is to say 'no sick Socrates exists'. The meaning of statements will be considered with greater detail in the treatise *On Propositions*.

11

1. Contraries in the fundamental sense are defined as the most different under the same genus or as the most distinct genera which cannot exist in

the same thing at the same time and with respect to the same thing (14a19-20, 23b22-3, 1018a25-31, 1055a3-29). Since to a given contrary there can be only one contrary (1055a19-21), contraries go in pairs. Hence the contrary of an evil cannot be sometimes an evil and sometimes a good unless it be with respect to two different things. Bravery, for example, with respect to its definition or its *substance* is a mean and lies between two extremes, cowardice and rashness, which are extremes and are therefore contraries; but with respect to excellence or what is best, bravery is an extreme and is contrary to both rashness and cowardice, which are extremes as vices. Thus rashness and cowardice taken together as a unit are furthest from what is best and form *as such* the contrary of bravery; so it is by being the worst that each of them is opposed to bravery as a contrary. 1106b36-7a7.

It appears, then, that the discussion here of good and bad as contraries can stand improvement.

2. The name 'contraries' here refers to the primary contraries, health and disease, not to Socrates in health and Socrates in disease as contraries, and the subject is Socrates. 1018a25-35.

3. By 'those contraries' he means the composite contraries, e.g., Socrates in health and Socrates in disease.

4. Contrary genera may come under a higher genus. Virtue and vice, for example, are contraries and are genera with species under them, but they are both habits.

5. Under what category do goodness and evil come? According to 1096a19-29, the good may be a substance, e.g., God, or a quality, e.g., a virtue, or a thing under any one of the other categories. If so, then how can the good be a genus? But the name 'genus' has more than one meaning. In a limited sense, 'genus' signifies either a category or a species (not ultimate) coming under just one category, though some exceptions are indicated in 11a20-38. But this is not the sense in which 'genus' is predicable of goodness; so 'genus' must be used in another and looser or wider sense (1004a4-5, 1004b33-5a1, 1024b10-6). Perhaps it is in this wider sense that 'cause', 'substance', 'matter', and other such philosophical names are called 'genera'.

12

1. It is not clear how the existence of one follows from that of two; for the word 'one' may be (a) either a name signifying a unit in a number (1016b17-25, 1052b14-24), in the number two here, or (b) a name predicable of a thing in any category (1003b33-4a5, 1053b20-1), for each thing is one. If sense (a) is taken, then a unit exists in two only potentially, not *actually*, and this qualification must be granted; if sense (b) is taken, the statement is true as it stands.

2. A demonstration presupposes principles from which it proceeds, and the principles of demonstration are terms, definitions, axioms, and hypotheses. Even in demonstrations, some theorems precede or are presupposed by others, as in geometry. Both principles and prior theorems are thus elements of later theorems. 71b19-2a24, 184a10-6.

3. In what way is a fact the cause of the corresponding truth? Now since truth in the primary sense exists only in the soul (for vocal and written statements are said to be true in a secondary sense), truth depends in some way on the soul and is thus caused, partly at least, by the soul; and since a fact must exist if the corresponding truth is to be intuited or demonstrated or become known in some other way, truth depends also on that fact and is thus caused, partly at least, by that fact. Truth, then, is caused partly by the fact and partly by the knower who grasps that fact and has that truth.

4. The manner in which priority is discussed in the *Metaphysics* (1018b9-19a14) is somewhat different from and superior to that in which it is discussed here. Here, the five senses of 'prior' are listed without any attempt to relate them generically or according to any principle; but in the *Metaphysics*, first a general statement is made (1018b9-12), something which reminds one of general statements concerning being, and then the different senses are given by the addition of qualifications to the general statement. Moreover, the fundamental sense of 'prior' here is stated to be that of time, which is an attribute of a substance and not a substance, but in the *Metaphysics* the main priority is assigned to a subject rather than to an attribute of it (1019a4-6), and, philosophically, the primary subject is a substance. In *Metaphysics*, then, the discussion of priority is superior in two ways. The unification of the various senses indicates a superiority in scientific method, and positing the primary sense of 'priority' to be that of a subject rather than that of an attribute or a predicate of it indicates a superiority in philosophical intuition. Clearly, then, the account on priority in the *Categories* was written earlier than that in the *Metaphysics*.

13

1. As in the case of 'prior', so here the fundamental sense of 'simultaneity' is assigned to time. Simultaneity is not considered in Book Δ of the *Metaphysics*.

2. The one-word Greek names corresponding to 'feathered', 'terrestrial', and 'aquatic' are nouns, and perhaps we should include 'animal' after each of the English adjectives, e.g., perhaps 'terrestrial animal' is the proper translation of the Greek word πεζόν, and likewise for the others.

3. No simultaneous existence is implied here. No one immediate species under a genus has any priority over another immediate species, and this

suggests that one may apply 'simultaneous by nature' to the various immediate species into which a genus is divided.

4. What would Aristotle say of two things which come into being at the same time but are not destroyed at the same time?

14

1. We have here another indication that this part of the *Categories* was written before the major works, i.e., before the *Metaphysics*, the *Physics*, the *Posterior Analytics*, and others. The word κίνησις (= 'motion') in the *Categories* is posited as a sort of genus of the six kinds which are listed, but in 200b33-4, 1069b9-13, and elsewhere the word μεταβολή (= 'change') is used instead, and κίνησις is limited to increase, decrease, alteration, and locomotion.

A problem arises as to whether the kinds of motion should be six or not. One may argue that generation and destruction are motions with respect to substance, increase and diminution are motions with respect to quantity, and therefore that the kinds of motion, generically taken, are those with respect to four categories, namely, substance, quantity, quality, and place. One may raise a further problem. If we are to posit the motions listed, whether six or four in kind, as being the fundamental motions, perhaps an argument is needed to show that motions with respect to the other six categories, if existing at all, are not fundamental but secondary or accidental. Perhaps such argument belongs to another treatise. 224a21-6b17, 246b10-7, 1068a8-b25, 1088a29-b1.

2. Perhaps 'move' should be used instead of 'alter', for none of the other motions is posited as being an alteration.

3. In 260a26-b7, it is shown that alteration presupposes locomotion, and this appears to contradict what is stated here—perhaps another indication that this part is an earlier work. It is possible for a body to alter without locomotion if the body as a whole remains in the same place, as in the case of a glass of wine which turns sour; but some of the parts of that body have to undergo locomotion if the body is to be altered. Thus in one sense a body may alter without locomotion, but in another sense it need not, and in each case the qualification just indicated should be made.

4. This is a strange example. All quantities are attributes of substances, and attributes have no physical matter and hence cannot move (193b22-35, 989b32, 1067b9-11). So how can a square, which is an attribute and has no physical matter, be increased? Does this indicate that this is an earlier work?

Now it would be true to say that a physical body which has a square form on one of its faces is not altered in shape—for shape is a quality

(10a11-6)—if (1) to it is attached another physical body having an appropriate form of a gnomon on one of its faces, as shown in the Figure, or if (2) it is increased uniformly when heated but keeps the same form. If we accept (1) there is still a difficulty. A body is increased if every part of it is increased (320a8-2a33). If so, then a square is not increased if a gnomon is added to it, unless we use 'increase' in another or a secondary sense. If so, then a thing is increased (a) in the primary or fundamental sense if every part of it is increased, but (b) in a secondary or qualified sense if the whole of it is increased but not in the primary or fundamental sense. Thus the example given here would be an increase in sense (b); and so would the increase of a body be, if only a part of it is increased but the other part is not changed with respect to quantity.

One may raise another related problem. Here, the contrary of the name 'increase' (= αὔξησις) is 'diminution' (= μείωσις), but in the other works it is 'decrease' (= φθίσις). If 'diminution' is the genus of 'decrease', as 320b30-1 suggests, then perhaps 'increase' has two senses, one generic and the other specific, like the names 'chance' and 'disposition'. Accordingly, the contrary of 'increase' in sense (a), which is the primary sense, would be 'decrease', but the contrary of 'increase' in sense (a) or (b) would be 'diminution'. Of course, there is a third contrariety. If 'increase' is taken in sense (b), then it will have its own contrary, and this would be, let us say, '*diminution*', which is the other species of 'diminution'.

In 226a31-2, increase is described as a motion in the direction of complete magnitude, and decrease as the contrary of such direction.

5. Perhaps motion without qualification is motion without regard to its kind or direction, and this would be just motion. Now just as the contrary of something belonging to a subject is not any contradictory but has the same subject to which it may belong as that to which its contrary may belong—e.g., both health and disease are contraries and belong to animals—so the contrary of motion as just motion should be that which may belong to the same subject to which motion itself may belong. But the contrary of motion as just motion in a subject which may be in motion is rest in that subject. Hence the contrary of motion as just motion should be rest.

6. Destruction is a qualified motion and has the direction (using 'direction' in a wide sense) from being to nonbeing, with physical matter as the underlying subject (224b8-9, 225a1-20), as in the case of the death of an animal. So its contrary would be generation, which is a motion in the direction from nonbeing to being, as in the case of the birth of an animal. Both destruction and generation are elsewhere said to be changes (i.e., what Aristotle here calls 'motions') with respect to substance, for there is a change of substance. Similar remarks apply to increase and diminution, which are said to be motions with respect to quantity. 1069b9-14.

But Aristotle seems somwhat uncertain as to what the contrary of locomotion is, and likewise for the contrary of alteration. First he posits rest with respect to place as the contrary of change with respect to place, then he adds a change to the contrary place as an alternative and says that this motion is most opposed to a motion with respect to place. He is even more uncertain as to what the contrary of alteration is, but he gives a similar account.

Now if the contrary of unqualified motion is rest, it seems that rest should be the contrary of locomotion not qua locomotion but qua motion, and rest with respect to place and change (or motion) with respect to place should be contraries not insofar as both are qualified but insofar as the first is rest and the second is motion. On the other hand, if we are to posit rest with respect to place as being the contrary of change (or motion) with respect to place, we should likewise posit (a) rest with respect to quantity as being the contrary of motion with respect to quantity, whether this motion be increase or diminution, and also (b) rest with respect to substance as being the contrary of motion with respect to substance, whether this motion be generation or destruction.

Further, increase and diminution are motions with respect to quantity and have contrary directions (using 'direction' in a wide sense), and they are posited as contraries; and generation and destruction are motions with respect to substance, and they, too, are posited as contraries. If so, then the same should apply to motions with respect to alteration and place, for motions with respect to these have contrary directions also. For example, upward motion is contrary to downward motion, and becoming hot is contrary to becoming cold.

It appears, then, that there should be some uniformity in all the above contraries. Perhaps direction should be the principle according to which both contraries should be posited as being motions. For just as 'being' is not a genus in the fundamental sense but each category is immediately a being (998b22-7, 1045a36-b7), so 'motion' and 'rest' should not be taken as genera in the fundamental sense but be regarded like 'being'. If so, then a motion with respect to a category is immediately a motion just as a category is immediately a being, and likewise for rest; and so the contrary of a motion with respect to a category should still be rest with respect to that category. In the case of generation, however, there seems to be a difficulty, for rest does not seem to apply. Generation is motion from nonbeing to being, and one may deny that nonbeing can be at rest. But the kind of nonbeing which becomes a being exists potentially, and one may argue that rest applies to such nonbeing, e.g., to the various materials which can become a house.

A more complete and detailed account of contrarieties in rest and motion, somewhat different from the account here, is given in the *Physics*, 229a7-231a17.

15

1. The expression 'to have' (or 'having') is not univocal. Senses (1) and (2) are close in meaning, for what is had is a quality or a quantity, and each of these is present in a substance as in a subject. Of course, one might use 'is virtuous' instead of 'having virtue', and 'is three cubits tall' instead of 'having a height of three cubits', for there is no difference in meaning, and there are similar alternatives in Greek. This usage may apply to other categories besides quantity and quality, but it depends on the particular language. In English we may use 'having a relation', as in 'having a certain ratio', and perhaps the same applies to other languages; e.g., ἔχειν λόγον is used in Greek.

From 1b25-2a3 it appears that sense (3) is the category of having (or possessing), or an example of it. In sense (4) that which is had by a thing is a part of the thing, and a part is not actually a thing but only potentially; so this sense is quite distinct from the others. Sense (5) appears to be the inverse relation of something which comes under the category of 'somewhere'; for example, if the jar has the wine, the wine is somewhere, in the jar. Senses (6) and (7) appear to indicate relations of substances to other substances.

In the *Metaphysics*, 1023a8-25, senses (6) and (7) above are left out, perhaps because of their unimportance, but other important senses are added, mainly those referring to the moving cause and to the cause as form. So it appears that the senses in the *Metaphysics* were formulated later.

ON PROPOSITIONS

Commentaries

1

1. From the contents it appears that this treatise is concerned with propositions and their attributes. The title Περί ‘Ερμηνίας, which may be translated as 'On Interpretation', is too wide and does not quite describe the contents; and I doubt that it is Aristotle's title. I have therefore chosen *On Propositions* as the title; for (a) nouns and verbs are parts of statements, (b) the various kinds of statements are like species of statements, if not strictly species, (c) relations between statements are properties or attributes of statements, (d) all statements are propositions or parts of propositions but not all propositions are statements, and (e) lines 17a1-7 suggest this title. An alternative to this title would be '*Statements*'; for, although some propositions may be regarded as wholes with statements as parts, such propositions may be regarded as combinations of statements or relations between statements, and such combinations or relations may be regarded as attributes or properties of statements. A synonym of the word 'proposition', we may add, is 'declarative sentence'.

2. Nouns and verbs are parts or elements of statements, and *as such* they are the material cause of statements. As elements, they are principles, and they are discussed first (16a19-b25); and this procedure is analogous to what is done in the *Physics* (Book A). Then follows a discussion of the formal cause or the form of statements. The sentence as a genus of a statement is considered first, then an indication is given as to the kinds of sentences to be considered (17a3-4), namely, those which are true or false. Such

sentences are called 'declarative', and they are either simple or not. Statements are simple declarative sentences, and two species of such statements, affirmations and denials, are mentioned. Relations between statements and kinds of statements, and also between these and the kinds of objects they signify, are briefly considered next.

3. This statement seems to suggest that spoken expressions among men precede written expressions, and hence that the latter are used as substitutes for the former. A sign of this is observed in children, for they first learn to speak and then to write.

4. Spoken and written expressions for the same mental impressions differ not only from one language to another, but also within the same language for different persons. It is assumed here that men have the same mental impressions for the same things, whether under the same conditions, or under different conditions if abstraction has been made. Sensations of the same thing from different positions differ, for the conditions are not the same; so if the corresponding mental impressions are to be the same, an abstraction must be assumed. For example, if a house at a distance is called 'house' by two men who observe it from different positions, their sensations of the house differ in some ways; but their impressions of the house merely as a house would not include the differences between their sensations of that house.

What does 'mental impression' exactly mean? Three distinctions arise. (a) One may think, without using any words in his thought, that John is running, and the thought or image of this in the soul is like the visual image of seeing John running. (b) One may think with both the words (as when one reads silently) and the corresponding thought or image. (c) One may think of the words, as when he reads silently, but not have any image of John running. Which of these three is a mental impression? Perhaps they are those indicated by (a); for, in (c), words differ from language to language, and such is the case in (b) also, though in (b) the thought or image is common even if different languages are used.

The difference between a symbol and a sign is not discussed here. One may read Kretzmann's *Aristotle On Spoken Sound Significant by Convention in Ancient Logic and Its Modern Interpretions*, 1974.

5. Since mental impressions are likenesses of things and spoken expressions are posited as symbols of mental impressions, perhaps 'spoken expressions' applies to nouns, verbs, and sentences. If so, then spoken expressions are vocal sounds, but vocal sounds are not necessarily spoken expressions. 420b5-10, 535a27-9.

In what sense are mental impressions likenesses of things? Using an analogy, but perhaps roughly, a picture of a tree is to that tree as a sensation of a tree is to that tree. But while pictures and sensations are limited to what is sensed, mental impressions include also thoughts which are universal, and the objects of thought need not be sensible. The word 'likeness', then, does not seem to be limited to what can be sensed. Now while it is appropriate to say that a picture of a tree is like a tree, since the sensation of the picture and that of the tree resemble each other, the resemblance between a sensation of a tree and the tree appears to be less close, if close at all; for one cannot sense a sensation. Yet there is a close relation between a sensation and the thing sensed in relation to that which senses it, a one-to-one correspondence, so to say, like the correspondence between a sensation and the thing sensed, and perhaps it is in view of this that, in the absence of a name, Aristotle uses 'likeness' instead of introducing a new name. Perhaps ὁμοίωμα is used in a wider sense than 'likeness'.

6. The word 'these' refers to mental impressions, which include sensations and images and other thoughts, all of which are discussed in *On the Soul*; perhaps 'these' refers also to the objects of these impressions as related to mental impressions, for these too are discussed there to some extent.

7. We may raise many problems concerning the meaning of lines 16a3-11, for it is very compressed. Perhaps Aristotle is stating only results here, for the discussion of such problems belongs to other disciplines, and much of Aristotle's work is lost; but in the absence of that discussion we are not even certain of what the results are. In view of this, I am adding, in the Appendix, Prof. John M. Crossett's translation and interpretation of lines 16a3-11.

8. A thought may be simply of a thing, e.g., of a triangle or Socrates or the number 7, or it may be of a thing as having an attribute, e.g., of the fact that Socrates was a philosopher, in which case truth or falsity would apply to that thought. The names 'truth' and 'falsity' apply to spoken and written expressions also, but in a secondary and analogous sense, for such expressions are symbols and are used for the sake of the corresponding thoughts. Since the correspondence between thoughts and the corresponding spoken or written expressions is one-to-one, no ambiguity arises in the use of the names 'truth' and 'falsity'.

9. The expression 'to be' is universal. When specified and applied to a goat-stag, it may take such forms as 'a goat-stag exists', 'a goat-stag is white', and 'a goat-stag did not exist'.

10. To qualify something is to restrict it in some way, and so what is unqualified has no restrictions. That which exists without qualification, then, would be that which is not limited by time but exists always, whether eternally or hypothetically. For example, the universe exists always and eternally (according to Aristotle), and 'all men are mortal' is true for every man, regardless of the time or place of his existence, even if any given individual does not exist eternally. In science, all statements of the form 'every A is B' or 'no A is B' signify things with unqualified existence, as in

the case of 'all vertical angles are equal'. But that which has temporal qualification is limited to a definite interval of time, whether present, past, or future. 34b7-8.

Perhaps the name 'goat-stag' is introduced because it appears to be somehow a composite of 'goat' and 'stag'; but such a composite by itself is not true or false, for there is no verb and no reference to time is indicated.

2

1. More explicitly, in the expression 'green field' the part 'field' has its own meaning. But 'field' in 'Greenfield', which is the name of a man, has no meaning of its own, for though it is a part of the name 'Greenfield', it is only a material part of that name.

The Greek names which Aristotle uses to illustrate his point may be translated as 'Goodhorse' and 'good horse', the first being the name of a man.

2. The parts 'black' and 'mail' in the name 'blackmail' suggest something black or ominous mailed to a person, but *literally* neither part necessarily signifies the meaning or part of the meaning of 'blackmail'. Blackmailing can be done without any mailing or the use of anything black.

The name which Aristotle uses in Greek is translated as 'pirate-boat', but we are using the word 'blackmail' in order to bring out the point which Aristotle has in mind.

3. That which exists or comes to be by nature exists either always or for the most part, and if not always, nature is impeded, as in the case of a baby born with six fingers. But no thing is by nature signified by a given name, for bread is signified by different names in different languages, and no name exists for a thing by nature or prior to the knowledge of that thing, as in the case of what is now called 'meson' or 'electron' or 'neutron'. In fact, we may choose any symbol to name a given thing, and to make such a choice is to make the choice by convention. 134a28-30, 199b14-8, 663b27-9, 847a14-6.

One might argue that since man by nature desires to understand, for he has the power of doing so and hence of *actualizing* that power, he eventually comes to use names and verbs and sentences; and such is actually the case. If so, then it is by nature that men use spoken expressions, and such expressions are natural and not conventional instruments. Even if we grant this, however, still it is not by nature that apples are called 'apples', for different people use different names for them. Thus particular names for particular things appear to be coined by convention, even if we grant that, in general, it is by nature that names are coined by man.

4. We might have chosen 'not man' instead of 'not-man', for there is no hyphen in the corresponding Greek names; but we chose 'not-man' to avoid the possibility of confusion.

What is the exact meaning of 'not-man', if it may belong as a predicate to what exists as well to what does not exist? For one thing, the statement 'Socrates is not-man' is false, if Socrates exists, but is the statement 'a square with unequal diagonals is not-man' true or false? The word 'is' has many senses, and perhaps in one of those senses some statements of the form 'A is B' are true if A does not exist, as in 'nonbeing is nonbeing'. Some definitions are needed to settle certain linguistic expressions.

5. In some manuscripts the Greek for 'since it may belong to what exists as well as to what does not exist' does not appear.

3

1. The literal translation is 'said of something else' or 'said with respect to something else'. This gives the appearance of indicating a said-of relation, which is considered in Section 2 of the *Categories* and discussed in Comm. 3 of that Section, but the expression is not always used in this way. Instead, we shall use 'said about', and this expression will be used as a genus to include both the said-of and the present-in relation, as indicated at the end of the paragraph. Thus in 'Socrates runs' the verb 'runs' indicates a present-in relation, but in 'red is a color' the verb 'is a color' indicates a said-of relation. The latter verb has three words, but it is considered as one name, like 'runs'; and just as 'runs' and 'is running' have the same meaning, so in Greek a verb may be stated as one word or as more than one word but still have the same meaning (21b9-10). If stated as one word, and perhaps such is what Aristotle has in mind here, then no part of it in virtue of its nature as a part has any meaning. If stated as more than one word, perhaps it resembles the composite noun 'blood-thirsty', like the noun 'blackmail', in which the part 'thirsty' gives the appearance of having meaning but does not, as a separate part, signify anything.

One may raise the question whether 'to be said about' has the same meaning as 'to belong'; perhaps it has a narrower meaning, for if A belongs to B, A may be predicated of B but not be said of B or be present in B.

2. The Greek has one word for 'is healthy'; so to bring out the point, we are using 'recovery' and 'recovers' instead of 'health' and 'is healthy', respectively.

3. The word πτῶσις applies to past or future tense but not to present tense; but in the absence of a corresponding English word, we translate it as 'tense', with the understanding that it does not apply to present tense.

4. The Greek expression for 'was healthy' is a single word, and so is the expression for 'will be healthy', and each word indicates a third person singular.

What about the verb in 'the universe is indestructible'? It signifies necessity or eternal time and is not limited to the present. The word 'is', of course, has several meanings, and one of the meanings of the verb in 'A is B' includes necessity or eternal time (89b36-90a23, 1051b9-22), if 'time' be the correct word here, as in 'man is mortal' and 'motion exists'.

5. An alternative to 'fact' is 'thing'.

4

1. Apparently, an utterance is simpler than a sentence; and perhaps it is a noun or a verb, whether definite or indefinite, as indicated later in 17a17-8. The example given is a noun. Is there any difference between an utterance and a name? Dionysius Thrax defines utterance as a noun or a verb in a syntactical context. Such a noun or verb differs from the entry in a dictionary. 17a17-20.

2. Affirmations and denials are declarative sentences, and these are species of sentences; so a sentence need not be an affirmation or a denial.

3. Perhaps the word 'is' here is used generically. In 'Socrates is', it is used without qualification, and 'Socrates is' in this sense has the same meaning as 'Socrates exists'; but Aristotle uses 'is' in a qualified sense also, without adding the predicate, and in this sense 'Socrates is' means Socrates is something, e.g., Socrates is healthy, or something of this sort. The word 'is' has many senses. 1017a7-b9.

4. Because of linguistic differences, we use the name 'virtue', instead of the name 'man'; for the point to be brought out depends partly on linguistic differences. No part of the noun 'virtue' signifies anything; and though the part 'use' in 'mouse' has meaning if used separately and not as a part, it has no meaning at all as a part of the name 'mouse'.

For Aristotle, we may add, the Greek word translated here as 'syllable' has a somewhat different meaning from what we call 'syllable'. 1456b34-7.

5. 16a22-7.

6. 16b26-8.

7. The Greek word ἀποφαντικός, translated as 'declarative', is derived from the Greek word translated as 'statement'. We shall use 'proposition' as a synonym for 'declarative sentence'.

5

1. What is the meaning of 'primarily one'? Of things in which there is priority according to some principle, there are cases in which one of the

things is first or primary, as in the case of positive integers ordered according to the principle of increase and so having 1 as first, Similarly, according to the principle of simplicity or presupposition, a proposition no part of which is a proposition is primary or first and so prior to such propositions whose forms are, in modern symbolism, p • q, p ⊃ q, and the like.

For Aristotle, the forms of an affirmation are 'A is B', 'every A is B', and 'some A are B', in which 'is B' and 'are B' are the verbs, and similarly when tenses of verbs are used. But the verb need not be expressed linguistically in this fashion; for one may use 'John walks' instead of 'John is walking'. Since B may be in any of the ten categories, the above forms exhaust all the kinds of affirmations. For example, in the affirmation '5 is greater than 3' the predicate 'greater than 3' signifies a relation; in 'Socrates is sick' the predicate signifies a quality; in 'Brutus killed Caesar' the predicate signifies an action; in 'Socrates is in the Agora' the predicate signifies somewhere; and in 'Socrates exists' the predicate signifies existence, though here one might raise the problem whether 'existence' is a predicate or not. Similar remarks apply to a denial.

Evidently, those who say that Aristotle is inadequate when he uses only the above forms to include all possible affirmations are mistaken; for the various categories as he describes them exhaust all kinds of predications and hence all those kinds of propositions of which each is primarily one but not one by conjunction. Relations as predicates are included, since the word 'predicate' for Aristotle is general and extends to all categories, as stated in 10b17-25. Linguistically, we may add, κατηγορεῖν (= 'to predicate') is derived from κατὰ and ἀγορεύειν, and its literal translation is 'to say something in accordance with'; and, of course, what may be said in accordance with a thing may be anything whatsoever which is true of it and is not limited to certain things which do or do not belong to it in one mode or another.

What about statements such as 'it is raining', 'there was a parade', and the like? Evidently, these are idiomatic expressions, and they can be replaced by 'rain drops fall', 'people marched on such and such an occasion', and so on, and the latter are more analytic and more subject to logical analysis than their idiomatic counterparts. The same applies to 'if A is B, then C is D', 'p implies q', and others. Other objections may be made as to Aristotle's adequacy, especially in connection with an adequate analysis of propositions for deduction, for modern analysis gives the appearance of being superior in many ways. An appraisal of such objections will be omitted here, for it requires, among other things, an accurate translation of *Prior Analytics*, along with the appropriate definitions, and also commentaries.

According to what principle is an affirmation primary or prior to a denial? Grammatically, an affirmation is simpler than a denial, for a denial is formed by the addition of the word 'not' to the affirmation or of some other equivalent. Ontologically and according to the principle of simplicity, an affirmation is prior to a denial; for an affirmation signifies a unity of two things, e.g., 'Socrates is healthy' signifies a healthy Socrates and a healthy Socrates is one thing, but a denial signifies no such unity but a separation of two things, and unity is prior to separation just as one is prior to two. 1018b9-9a14.

2. What kinds of declarative sentences are one by conjunction? From Aristotle's remarks about conjunction, here and elsewhere, it is not easy to give a definite answer. The *Iliad* or any novel would be one by conjunction (93b35-6, 1030b8-10, 1045a12-4), and so would such expressions as 'he came and spoke', 'he came, spoke, and left', 'if it rains, it is wet', and the like (1407b37-8a1); for in all these there is some continuity in thought and the parts are somehow connected or unified. Declarative sentences are many, on the other hand, if they are not joined or cannot be joined or do not indicate or signify something which is one (17a15-7, 18a18-26).

Would Aristotle say that the expression '5 is odd, and Socrates was wise', which is of the form $p \cdot q$ in modern terms, is one declarative sentence? Perhaps not. For if 'A' is equivocal, he considers 'A is B' as many (18a18-26), and 'A is B' in this case has the form $p \cdot q$ in which p and q have the same subject. The word 'and', then, would not be sufficient to make $p \cdot q$, in which p and q are declarative sentences, one declarative sentence. The form $p \cdot q$, of course, may be one by accident (1015b16-36).

If such be Aristotle's position, would he not be inadequate in his logic? Perhaps he would say that dealing with unities such as $p \cdot q$ (in which p and q are not one by conjunction) is dealing with accidents, and that such is not the concern of the philosopher or the scientist in general. 1027a20-1.

3. The word 'definition' has two senses; it means the definiens, like 'a rational animal', or the combination of definiens and definiendum, e.g., 'man is a rational animal'. The first sense is meant here.

4. The names 'one' and 'many' are metaphysical; hence discussions concerning oneness and plurality belong to metaphysics and not to the nature of propositions or to grammar. We may suggest the nature of the problem by using an example.

Let A be 'a triangle is a magnitude', B be 'a triangle is a continuous quantity', C be 'a triangle is continuous', D be 'a triangle is a quantity', and let a magnitude be defined as a continuous quantity. Is A one statement, and is B one statement? Now A states just what B states, though B states it in a different way, i.e., analytically; but B appears to state what C and D together state and so B appears to be two statements. Hence A appears to be two statements. Moreover, if 'continuous' in C is definable, C itself may be replaced by C_1, just as A may be replaced by B; and since C_1 thus appears to be more than one statement, A will ultimately appear to be more than two statements. This process may continue. The solution to this problem is given in the *Metaphysics*, 1037b8-8a35.

5. A denial, too, indicates one object; for the statement '5 is not even' indicates one fact: the fact that 5 is not even, or else the denial that 5 is even (and a denial is one object).

6. An alternative to 'are not conjoined' is 'cannot be conjoined'.

7. The word 'simple' appears to be redundant, for a statement is simple according to 17a20. Is the word 'simple' used for emphasis? The difficulty is removed if we translated as follows: 'The simple [proposition], which is a statement, is a vocal sound . . . time'. The order of the words in Greek is unusual.

8. The word ὑπάρχειν (= 'to exist') is taken in the general sense, and this sense covers what is signified by statements such as 'Socrates exists', 'Socrates is wise', 'all men are virtuous', and 'some men are virtuous'; for another way of saying that Socrates is wise is to say that wise Socrates exists. For Aristotle, we may add, 'all men are virtuous' would be false if no man can exist.

An alternative to 'signifying the existence or nonexistence of something' is 'signifying that something belongs or does not belong to something else'.

9. Do the divisions of time include more than past, present, and future? If 'all vertical angles are equal' is a statement with 'are equal' as the verb, then necessity (or eternal time, if you wish) will have to be one of the divisions of time; for some facts are necessarily true and are not limited by time. See Commentary 4 of Section 3.

6

1. For the meaning of 'to exist', see Comm. 8 of the preceding Section.

2. The word 'opposite' here means the contradictory. Thus the opposite of 'every A is B' is 'not every A is B', and the opposite of 'no A is B' is 'some A are B'.

3. Alternatives to 'contradiction' are 'two contradictories' or 'contradictories'.

4. If 'A' or 'B' has one meaning in 'every A is B' but another in 'not every A is B', then these may be both true or both false; and one may hold that two contradictories may be both true or both false, contrary to the principle of contradiction. But the argument is sophistic; for, in view of the equivocation, the two statements are not contradictory. For example, one may say that both 'every triangle has its angles equal to two right angles' and its denial may be true, for the first statement is true in Euclidean geometry

and its denial is true in Lobachevsky's geometry. But there is an equivocation, for the word 'triangle' has different meanings in the two statements. Aristotle discusses sophistical arguments in his *Sophistical Refutations*, 164a20-184b8.

7

1. The usual translation of πρᾶγμα is 'thing' or 'fact', words which need not signify a name, but there is a difficulty; for if the word 'predicable' which follows has the same meaning as that in the *Categories*, the things which are predicable will have to be names, and that which is a universal or an individual will have to be a name, like 'man' or 'Callias'. Then this sense of the word 'universal' would be different from that in the *Categories*, for it would apply to a name and not to what the name signifies; and similarly for the word 'individual'. Is 'predicable' used in a different sense here?

The word καθόλου (= 'universal') is an abbreviation of the two words κατὰ and ὅλου, and these two words taken together are translated as 'of all' or 'with respect to all'. Accordingly, if 'predicable' has the same meaning here as in the *Categories*, an alternative translation would be: 'Some things are [predicable] of all [things of a kind] but others [are predicable] of an individual'. The things which are predicable, of course, would have to be names (see *Categories*, Comm. 1 of Section 3). Since the treatise here is concerned with propositions, one may be inclined to favor this translation, for propositions have names as parts, and the discussion of names comes under this treatise.

The expression 'a square circle' raises another difficulty. Since it signifies nonbeing, which is neither one nor many, can it be used as a subject or a predicate in a statement if a predicate is by nature predicable either of many or of one thing? The meaning of 'individual' in line 17a40 is given in a negative way, i.e., as that which is not predicable of many, and, logically, that which is not predicable of many may be predicable either of one or of none. Thus 'Socrates is a square circle' and 'a square circle is a quantity' would be statements; but to call an expression 'individual' even if it is not predicable of anything is to use it in an unusual sense. Callias is given as an example of an individual, but no example is given of nonbeing as an individual. But if an individual is not predicable of nonbeing (at least of that nonbeing which is impossible to be, like an eternal cat), expressions such as 'equilateral triangles with unequal medians do not exist' and 'an odd number which is divisible by 2 is an even number' would not be statements.

Expressions signifying nonbeing, we may add, give rise to many sophistical problems, and Aristotle was quite aware of this. The expression 'nonbeing is nonbeing' was often used (1030a25-6), and this is an affirmation, which appears to make nonbeing a thing; but one may use the denial 'nonbeing is not being' and so avoid this sophistical problem. Evidently, there is no one-to-one correspondence between language and things; for language may signify nonbeing also, and nonbeing is not a thing, except in a qualified way, e.g., when nonbeing as something potential, like a house 150 stories high, may come into existence.

2. The word 'white' is affirmed of man in 'man is white', but not universally of every man. So if something is affirmed of a universal subject universally, it is affirmed of every instance of that subject; and the subject of the statement will take the form 'every A', as in 'every A is B'. Similarly, if 'white' is denied universally of the subject, the subject of the statement will take the form 'no A', as in 'no A is B'.

Since contraries are most different within a genus, 'no A is B' will be the contrary of 'every A is B'; for the contradictory of 'every A is B' is 'not every A is B' (or 'some A are not B'), and 'not every A is B' differs less from 'every A is B' than 'no A is B' does since some A may be B when not every A is B. 1055a3-33.

3. When one truly says 'man is pale', it is possible for every man to be pale, and when he truly says at another time 'man is not pale', it is possible for no man to be pale; so the facts indicated may be contrary, although it is also possible for them not to be contrary, as when some men are pale and some are not pale, whether at the same time or at different times.

4. Alternatives to 'man is white' and 'man is not white' are 'men are white' and 'men are not white', respectively; for we often use the plural, as in 'men are selfish' and 'men are not saints'.

5. Does this statement posit a definition? If so, then the word 'contradictories' would be limited to statements with universal subjects and would not apply to statements with subjects which signify individuals, like 'Socrates is wise'. So it appears that the statement does not posit a definition but asserts that certain kinds of pairs of statements will be called 'contradictories'. See also Commentary 16.

One might argue that 'men are not white', too, is not universally taken and therefore that it is opposed to 'every man is white' in a contradictory way. But such is not what Aristotle means, as shown by the examples which he gives. To say that the denial of 'every A is B' is not universally taken is to deny the universality of 'every A is B', and this amounts to saying 'not every A is B'.

6. Literally, the translation should be 'there is a white man'; but we shall use the more common expression 'some men are white', and this should be understood as not excluding the case when only one man is white.

7. A universal affirmation has the form 'every A is B'; a universal denial

has the form 'no A is B'. What about 'every John is mortal'? The name 'John' signifies an individual man, and if there are many men who are called 'John', the name is used equivocally. So the expression 'every John is mortal' is either nonsense or many statements.

8. What was stated in Comm. 5 applies here also. The sentence does not posit a definition but asserts a fact. This fact follows from the definition of contraries; for contraries are most different within a genus (1055a3-33), and such can be shown to be the case here.

9. For Aristotle, the word 'is' in 'every A is B' signifies, besides the unity of B with A, also the existence of that unity. So if A does not exist, 'every A is B' will be false, and if A exists, the truth of 'every A is B' will imply the falsity of 'no A is B'. And if a man thinks that a nonexistent object is one, he is mistaken, for what really exists as one is not the object itself but his concept of it. It follows from these remarks, then, that 'every A is B' and 'no A is B' cannot be true at the same time. For modern logic, on the other hand, no such existence is signified by 'is' in 'every A is B' and in 'no A is B', and from this, 'every A is B' and 'no A is B' can be true at the same time. For example, 'every A is B' for modern logic means: for every instance x, if x is an A, then x is a B. Thus if there is no x which is an A, then there is no x which is an A and is not a B, and so 'if x is an A, then x is a B' is not false. As the mathematicians would say, if A is a null class, like the class of all triangles whose altitudes are not concurrent, then 'every A is B' is vacuously true or vacuously satisfied.

Both schools of thought are logically right, for whether they are right or not depends on how they use the word 'is'; so any criticism of Aristotle or of modern logic should be based not on logical principles but on usefulness or value or adequacy or some other such principle.

10. The expression 'universally taken' here is opposed to 'not universally taken' in the sense stated and exemplified in lines 17b6-12, i.e., to statements such as 'men are selfish' and 'men are not selfish', which are not universally taken, and not to statements such as 'some men are selfish' and 'not every man is selfish'. The last two are denials of 'no man is selfish' and 'every man is selfish', respectively, and it appears that these denials, too, are included among statements whose subjects are universally taken. We may call them 'particular' (not 'individual') to distinguish them from the other two.

11. The word 'man' may or may not be universally taken, as in 'every man is mortal' and in 'man is selfish'. But no such thing is possible in the case of 'Socrates' since the expression 'every Socrates' is nonsense if the word 'Socrates' is used univocally. Hence any predicate, say 'white', is related to 'Socrates' only in two opposed ways, as in 'Socrates is white' and 'Socrates is not white'.

12. It is not yet clear whether he regards such a pair as contradictories or not, but lines 17b38-8a12 which follow indicate that he does. See Comm. 16.

13. The statement 'men are white' is true if some or all men are white, and 'men are not white' is true if some men are not white or if no man is white. So both these statements are true if some men are white and some are not.

14. The argument is not spelled out; perhaps it amounts to the following. If some men are noble, and if the rest are in the process of becoming noble and are not disgraceful, both statements 'men are noble' and 'men are not noble' are still true.

15. The Greek is very abbreviated, and if expanded, its translation will be: 'But if that which the denial denies is different from that which the affirmation affirms, or if the subject of which something is denied in the denial is different from the subject of which something is affirmed in the affirmation'. We have used a shorter translation.

16. We have given a slightly expanded translation of the first part of (c), for the literal translation 'not every contradiction is true or false' may be confusing.

The problem indicated in Commentaries 5 and 12 may now be considered.

(1) If in line 18a11 the word ἀντίφασις (translated as 'contradictories') is correct, then also 'men are white' and 'men are not white' would be contradictories (lines 17b29-8a7, Comm. 12), and some contradictories would be true at the same time. Further, (a) the subject to which something may or may not belong (lines 17a25-37) may be universal but not universally taken, as in 'men are white'; (b) the sentence in lines 17b16-8 would not be a definition of 'in a contradictory way' but would merely state that the pairs indicated are opposed in a contradictory way (i.e., that they are contradictories), and this opposition would not necessarily exclude other kinds of pairs from being contradictories; and (c) opposite statements with an individual as a subject, like 'Socrates is white' and 'Socrates is not white', would be regarded as contradictories (lines 17b27-8, Comm. 11).

Now if some pairs of contradictories are true, what will happen to the principle of contradiction, which is considered in *Metaphysics*? If this difficulty is to be avoided, then either (a) the word 'contradictories' in the *Metaphysics* is defined for and applied to only statements whose subjects are individual or of the form 'every A' or 'no A', in which case we exclude universal subjects which are not universally taken, as in 'men are white' and 'men are not white', or (b) the expression τῷ αὐτῷ, which signifies a subject in the principle of contradiction (1005b19-20), cannot signify a universal which is not universally taken.

But does the principle of contradiction apply to statements or to things in general? The *Metaphysics* is concerned with being (or things) in general (1003a21-32); and the principle of contradiction applies primarily to all things, individually taken, and secondarily to statements. This is also evident from the way in which the principle is stated, namely, 'it is impossible for the same [object] to belong and not to belong to the same [object] at the same time and in the same respect'. 1005b19-20.

(2) Perhaps the word in line 18a11 should be ἀντίθεσις (translated as 'opposites') and not ἀντίφασις (translated as 'pair of contradictories'); but ἀντίθεσις appears less likely to be the case, for 'opposites' would be too general and would not state the cause, and this generality would yield no further gain over the less general word 'contradictories'. Aristotle's usual method, discussed in *Posterior Analytics*, is to state the cause.

One may raise another problem. If some men are white and some are not white, then both 'men are white' and 'men are not white' are true at the same time. But does 'men' signify the same thing (or things) in the two cases? Grammatically, it appears that it does, but the individuals of which 'white' is predicable in the first case are not those of which it is predicable in the second, for the men who are white are not the men who are not white, and the two sets of men are mutually exclusive. Accordingly, the expression 'the same thing' requires qualification. For 'men' appears the same grammatically in the two statements; but the things to which it applies are not the same, otherwise the two statements would not be true at the same time.

8

1. Statements with individual subjects, such as 'Socrates is wise', are also included; for in such statements something which is one is affirmed or denied of one subject, and the subject comes under 'or not', that is, the subject is not a universal taken universally.

But does 'not-man' signify one thing in the statement 'a cat is not-man'? According to Aristotle, 'not-man' signifies something which is one *in a sense* (19b8-10), perhaps because in the above statement, which is an affirmation, the predicate signifies the absence of one thing (of the nature of man) from a cat, which is assumed as existing, and that absence is one thing.

2. The statement 'coats are white' signifies nothing at all if 'coat' is posited to signify, not two things, but an object which is both a man and a horse; and we may use the expression 'man-horse' or 'man, horse' for such an object in this case. (By 'an object' we mean either a thing or nonbeing; and nonbeing may be possible, like a building 200 stories high, or impossible, like what we call 'a square with unequal diagonals' or like a man-horse). But problems arise, as we have indicated in Comm. 1 of Section 7.

If a statement, whether an affirmation or a denial, is posited by Aristotle to be one (or simple) when and only when it signifies one thing about one thing, then the statement 'a man-horse is white' is not simple; for 'a man-horse' cannot signify one thing since no thing can be both a man and a horse, although the grammatical form 'a man-horse' might lead someone to think that what is signified is something which is one, like a centaur in mythology. One might then object to Aristotle's position as not being adequate, for Aristotle would exclude 'X is Y' from being a simple statement if X or Y cannot exist; and we do use such expressions, whether (a) intentionally, or (b) hypothetically, that is, if we are not sure of whether X or Y exists or can exist but posit it to exist for purposes of investigation, as chemists and physicists do in the case of atoms and their parts. Moreover, would Aristotle exclude also 'X is Y' from being a simple statement if, when that expression is made, X or Y does not exist but can exist? For if X does not exist, it is not one. For example, would Aristotle posit as a subject a building 200 stories high, and would he deny that 'Socrates is wise' is a simple statement, now that Socrates is dead?

We may answer, the words 'being' (or 'thing') and 'one' have many senses (1015b16-7b9), and being and one imply each other (1003b22-31, 1054a13-9, 1061a15-8); and a thing may exist *actually* or potentially (an object has potential existence if it is possible for it to exist). So if X and Y are existing *actually*, then 'X is Y' is a simple statement, but if one of them exists potentially, or both of them exist potentially, then we must qualify the expression 'X is Y' and say, for example, that it is a simple statement potentially but not *actually*.

Aristotle does not have to worry about names such as 'man-horse' in a science, as he defines science; for demonstrated truth is the aim of scientific investigation, and all the names in such a science signify objects which are known to exist, either directly, e.g., by intuition or by sensation, or indirectly, e.g., by demonstration, as in the case of a triangle whose construction can be demonstrated. So statements such as 'X is Y' in which X or Y is a nonbeing do not arise. 71b9-2b4, 76a31-6.

But do we not use hypotheses such as Newton's First Law of Motion, even if no body exists which is not subject to a force? Now the First Law is not needed; for one may substitute another law, one which posits every body to be subject to a force, and still get the same results. Thus one may posit that the change in velocity of a body in motion depends in a certain way upon the force on that body. In fact, this is what the equation $F = ma$ does, and the First Law is unnecessary. But are all scientific laws like Newton's First Law subject to similar changes? If not, a logical difficulty arises; for it would then be possible in a science dealing with facts to demonstrate what exists or is possible to exist from a hypothesis which signifies what cannot exist (or, as some say, from a hypothesis which is vacuously true). But do straight lines and other such things exist, whether *actually* or potentially? If not, then geometry is not concerned with what exists, or not all geometry is concerned with what exists (for not all geometrical objects are ideal), and then one would find it difficult to explain why the applications of geometry to what exists are very accurate. Certainly, it is not by accident, for what is accidental happens infrequently, whereas the applications of geometry are always very accurate. We shall discuss in detail geometrical objects in the *Posterior Analytics* (Aristotle's philosophy of science).

In ordinary discourse, it seems that one gains in generality by regarding as simple statements also such forms as 'X is Y' in which X or Y or both cannot exist. Whether one chooses such generality or Aristotle's less general form of a simple statement is a matter of taste or of value. If it is known that X or Y cannot exist, perhaps Aristotle would find it useless to consider the forms 'X is Y' and 'X is not Y', for to do so would be playing games with impossibilities; and the gain in generality would be a gain with respect to impossibilities, if such be a gain at all. Aristotle is primarily concerned with being, whether simple or composite. And his concern with nonbeing is mainly with composite nonbeing, such as XY, which may be expressed by the statement 'X is Y', and in which X and Y are beings; for if it is known that X is impossible, why bother with XY, which may be even more impossible (if we are allowed to use this expression), or why bother with 'X is not Y', even if this expression is true? So Aristotle, if such is his position, may regard 'X is Y' or 'X is not Y' as not signifying anything or as being of no use because 'X' does not signify an *actual* or possible thing to begin with. On the other hand, if it is not known that X or Y cannot exist, then there is reason to regard 'X is Y' as a statement even if X should turn out to be impossible; for one might regard 'X is Y' as dialectical and subject to investigation, and dialectics is useful. So there are arguments for both sides.

Finally, another interpretation may be mentioned, one which we regard as unlikely. The literal translation of line 18a13 is: 'A statement is one affirmation or one denial if it signifies (or indicates) one about one, . . .'. Usually, the word σημαίνειν means to signify, but sometimes it is used by Aristotle in some other allied sense; e.g., perhaps it means to indicate, in a broad sense. One might then interpret him to be saying that a statement is one affirmation or one denial if it affirms or denies one predicate (which is a name and not what that name signifies) of one subject (which is also a name). If so, the problem of what a predicate is and what a subject is still remains.

3. The contradictory of 'every X is white' is 'not every X is white'; so if 'X' has two meanings, man and also horse, then 'every X is white' would be 'every man is white' and 'every horse is white', and 'not every X is white' would be 'not every man is white' and 'not every horse is white'. If every

man is white and no horse is white, then 'every X is white' with its double meaning will be false, and so will 'not every X is white'. One might interpret 'not every X is white' as being 'not every man and every horse is white', and if so, then one contradictory is true and the other false; but this is not Aristotle's meaning here.

9

1. As indicated in the next sentence, 'to be true, or to be false' does not necessarily mean that, of two contradictories, one must be true and the other false, for, as stated in 17b26-33, contradictories like 'men are white' and 'men are not white' may be both true; what it means is that the truth or falsity of a statement is already determined and cannot change.

2. 17b29-33.

3. A future particular may be stated in such terms as 'A will be', 'A will not be', 'A will be B', etc., in which A is an individual and not eternal, like Socrates or a certain house or a possible individual which might be but is not yet.

What about universals in the future? But a universal is of what exists always and everywhere, whereas the future puts a limitation on time. For example, the statement 'all vertical angles are equal' is true always and everywhere. Even a statement such as 'all Americans will get the flu next month' is not a universal, for there is a limitation at least with respect to time; and expressions such as 'all Americans' are qualified universals, if universals at all, for to be an American is an accident of a man. 87b32-3, 96a8-15.

4. Why is it not similar? For of the two statements 'A will be B' and 'A will not be B', too, one of them will be true and the other false.

But there is a difference between 'A is B' and 'A will be B' with respect to their *actual* truth or falsity, if we assume here that A is a destructible individual. The statement 'A is B' is definitely true, or definitely false, for at the time the statement is made, A is *actually* B, or A is *actually* not B, and nothing can change that *actuality*, whichever it is (19a23-4); and the same may be said of the past. For (a) what has happened is now definite, and both at present and in the future it has no longer the potentiality of not having happened, although before its occurrence it had the potentiality of happening or of not happening; and the same applies to (b) what has not happened but might have happened, for (b) too is definite. So since Aristotle is trying to refute what we may call 'determinism', it is not the determinism of what now exists or what already existed that concerns him—for what exists or existed cannot be changed—but the determinism of future facts or their opposites concerning destructible individuals. Accordingly, possible facts concerning such individuals in the future differ from similar *actual* facts of the present and the past, since it is not definite whether the former will come to be or not. And, according to Aristotle, those facts are indefinite not because we do not know all the past and present facts, but because we cannot know all the required facts which will cause a future fact; for, to know whether such a fact will be or will not be, one must have also principles which do not yet exist but will exist, such as someone's intention or *action* in the future. Possible facts in the future are indefinite, then, because some of their causes are future principles which, as principles, cannot be demonstrated from other principles and so from all the facts of the past and present, even if all the past and present facts were known by the demonstrator. For example, Aristotle maintains that, at time T, what a man decides to do cannot be demonstrated from all the events prior to T, and hence that every future decision is a principle and not a theorem. In short, Aristotle rejects the kind of determinism which maintains that complete knowledge of the present implies complete knowledge of the future.

The determinism which is based on physics alone would be refuted by Aristotle by the use of principles in the *Posterior Analytics*. For if A_1, A_2, . . .,A_m are the indefinable terms proper to physics and B_1, B_2, . . ., B_n are those proper to human conduct, e.g., to ethics, no definition or axiom or hypothesis proper to physics will have any of the B's as an indefinable term, and so no conclusion from the principles of physics would have any of the B's as a part. Accordingly, such a statement as 'John will be pleased tomorrow at 10 a.m.' cannot be demonstrated from the principles of physics alone, for pleasure cannot be defined in terms of the A's alone. Such is true even if certain states of physical particles correspond to pleasure; for a correspondence between a set of A's in some relation and a set of B's in some other relation makes the first set related to the second but is not identical to it, and reduction requires identity. Pleasure as a sensation, according to Aristotle, cannot be reduced to motions of particles alone; at most, such motions would be the material cause only, but pleasure has other kinds of causes in its definition also. Evidently, then, ethics cannot be reduced to physics. And if one wishes to use a more inclusive set of principles for determinism, that is, one which includes all the A's and all the B's and others also, other kinds of difficulties will arise; e.g., to mention two of them, the science which is to include both the A's and the B's will not be just physics, and all the terms of a science are universal, even when initial conditions are imposed, as in certain theorems and problems in physics and mathematics. For example, if a physicist says 'Let a sphere of radius 10 feet have a temperature of 100 degrees Centigrade at time T etc.', he means any sphere of radius 10 feet and a temperature of 100° C and at any time T, so his statement is universal. 75a38-b20.

5. This protasis will lead to absurd conclusions and will be rejected later, starting with 19a7; it includes statements concerning the future and appears to assume that such statements are at present definitely true or definitely false.

6. The principle of contradiction applies to the future particulars also.

7. What is stated from 18a39 to here is true, for only statements concerning present facts are considered. But from now on he generalizes to include statements concerning the future, and he does so purposely in order to bring out the absurdities.

8. An argument from what has happened is more convincing than an argument about what will or might happen, and Aristotle uses this sophistical device to make a strong case for the upholders of determinism concerning future events. The analogy is as follows: present facts are to true past statements concerning them as future facts are to present true statements concerning them.

Why the present tense in the expression 'it is'? Perhaps because of the different ways in which one may speak about future events. One may say 'X will be', or he may say "the statement 'X will be' is true", and the latter has the general form 'it is' or 'A is B'.

9. That which comes to be in either of two ways differs from that which comes to be by chance; for that which comes to be by chance happens occasionally, e.g., finding a dollar when going to the market, whereas in the case of that which comes to be in either of two ways, the relative frequency of each of the two alternatives is left unspecified.

10. If both an affirmation and its denial were false, then it would be possible for a thing neither to be nor not to be, and the principle of the excluded middle would be violated; for example, both 'it will rain tomorrow' and 'it will not rain tomorrow' would be false.

11. It is not clear why two attributes are used instead of just one, and how the arguments in this and the next sentence contribute to the main argument. The text is too abbreviated and perhaps corrupt, and I am not sure of its correct translation.

12. The word 'necessary' here signifies a necessity for a given affirmation (or denial) to be definitely true, or definitely false, regardless of the time it is made; otherwise there would be no point to the statement at all.

13. These are the future principles already discussed in Comm. 4 of this Chapter.

14. The potentiality both of being and of not being, of course, does not necessitate the possibility of being and of not being at the same time; in fact, such possibility is excluded because of the principle of contradiction, which states that it is impossible to be and not to be *at the same time.*

15. The decision, whether present or future, to cut the coat to pieces or

not to cut it, or to wear it till it is worn out is a principle according to Aristotle, and as a principle it cannot be demonstrated (or determined) from any other facts.

16. This is another way of saying that, if a thing now exists, say in the time interval (t_1, t_2), it is impossible for its existence during that interval to be truly denied now or in the future. In other words, once a thing happens, that happening cannot be undone. And if a thing occurred in the past, say during (T_1, T_2), that occurrence during this interval, too, cannot be undone. Similarly for objects which do not now exist or did not occur. So the necessity of the existence of a thing, when it exists, or of the nonexistence of a thing, when it does not exist, is hypothetical and hence qualified; it is not an unqualified necessity like that of the equality of vertical angles, for vertical angles are always and of necessity equal.

Things whose existence is necessary without qualification are things which exist of necessity and are not limited by time. For example, sums of equals are of necessity equal in all cases, the base angles of an isosceles triangle are of necessity equal in all cases, and motion exists of necessity and always. 251b19-28.

17. In other words, just as necessity with respect to being or nonbeing is of two kinds, qualified and unqualified, so necessity with respect to statements (or logical necessity, if you wish) is of two kinds. For example, if P, which does not exist always, exists now, then (a) it necessarily exists now, and (b) 'P exists now' is necessarily true; and both necessities are qualified. Similarly, if P does not exist now but might have existed or may exist, then it is necessary for P not to exist now and 'P does not exist now' is necessarily true; and both necessities are qualified by time, for P does not exist always. Again, vertical angles are equal of necessity, and 'vertical angles are equal' is necessarily true; but here both necessities are unqualified, for it is impossible for vertical angles not to be equal.

One may raise the problem whether Aristotle uses 'necessary' with the same meaning when he applies it to objects and to propositions; for, although the correspondence between necessity in objects and necessity in the corresponding propositions is one-to-one, correspondence may not be sameness. The meanings of 'necessary' are given in 1015a20-b15, for necessity has universal application and so its discussion belongs to metaphysics, and it appears that the word 'necessary' is not used univocally, even for objects. Lines 1015b11-2 suggest that there is (a) an order of priority in those meanings and (b) a primary and fundamental meaning; so perhaps the word 'necessary' is like the word 'being', which has many but related or analogous meanings, one of which is fundamental and primary. 1003a33-b18, 1017a7-b9.

18. Perhaps this part of the statement is general and applies to every object at any time, whether present, past, future, and even to objects which

necessarily exist or do not exist. The part which follows is the one at issue.

19. He is referring to objects which have the potentiality of being and of not being in the future, like a coat with respect to its being cut or not being cut tomorrow; for, as stated in Commentaries 16 and 17, there is no problem if an object exists of necessity or existed of necessity, whether without qualification or not, or if the object does not or did not exist in the same way. Now concerning such an object one cannot now truly say 'it will exist of necessity' or 'it will not exist of necessity'; or else, if one says that the object will exist, his statement cannot have the unqualified necessity of the statement 'the object will either be or not be', even if the object will come to be. For the statement 'an object will either be or not be' is always true and for all cases, but each of the former statements can never be true.

20. This necessity follows from the principle that of two contradictories concerning individuals, or concerning universals taken universally, one must be true and the other false, if both contradictories refer to the same time, whether past, present, future, or eternal.

21. Perhaps 'more likely to be true' means that past statements concerning similar objects were more often true than false, or that the present circumstances favor the occurrence of the object, or something of this sort.

22. For existing things, present or past, see Commentary 16.

10

1. It is not clear whether the objects in the affirmation are meant to be the subject and the predicate, which are parts of the affirmation, or what these signify. We are translating according to the first alternative.

2. 16a30-3, b12-5.

3. The verbs in 'man recovers' and 'man is recovering' are 'recovers' and 'is recovering', respectively, and they have the same meaning but differ linguistically. Since no name exists for the word 'is' in 'man is recovering', Aristotle says that it may be called 'a noun' or 'a verb'; but it differs from a verb as first defined and is not like the verb in 'man is'. The same applies to 'is' in 'man is just'.

4. In other words, two of the statements have 'not-just' as a predicate, and the other two have 'just' as a predicate; and 'not-just' is the privation of 'just'.

5. For convenience, the quotation marks are omitted from the statements in this and the later Diagrams or Tables.

6. 51b36-2a17.

7. What does 'every man is not-just' mean, and how does it differ from

'no man is just'? For one thing, 'every man is not-just' is an affirmation, in spite of the negative predicate 'not-just'; and if that affirmation is true, men exist, and none of them is just, so 'no man is just' will be true also. But in view of 13b27-35, if no man exists, 'every man is not-just' will be false but 'no man is just' will be true.

8. In the previous case, (a) and (c) may be both true at the same time, e.g., when some men are just and some are not; and so can (b) and (d). But whereas (A) and (C) can never be true at the same time, (B) and (D) can sometimes be true at the same time, e.g., when some men are just and some are unjust.

9. An alternative to 'by themselves' is 'in virtue of their nature'.

10. If 'X' is any chance predicate, from the truth of, say, 'every man is X' nothing can be said about the truth or falsity of 'every not-man is X' or of 'every not-man is not X'. So the subject must be the same if relations such as those in the diagrams are to exist. For example, from the truth of 'Socrates is good' nothing can be said about the truth or falsity of 'not-Socrates is good' or 'not-Socrates is not good', for not-Socrates may be a virtue or a vice.

11. Literally, the Greek word ὑγιαίνει translates into 'is healthy', which is composed of two words and contains the word 'is'. So to bring out the point as stated in Greek we use 'recovers', which is one word and does not contain the word 'is'.

12. See Comm. 9 of Section 7.

13. If 'some men are just' is true, there is a just man; and if there is a just man, then 'every man is not-just' is false and hence its contradictory 'not every man is not-just' is true.

14. If 'Socrates is not-wise' is to follow from 'Socrates is not wise', then the existence of Socrates must be assumed. Now this assumption is made in the phrase 'concerning an individual' in line 20a24, for an object which is an individual is one and exists. 1003b22-31, 1054a13-9.

15. Perhaps what is meant is that 'every man is not-wise' may be false or that its truth does not follow from the fact that 'every man is wise' is not true.

16. There seems to be a problem. The contrary of 'every man is wise' is given as 'every man is not-wise', but according to 17b20-3, it should be 'no man is wise'. Now 'no man is wise' follows from 'every man is not-wise', but 'every man is not-wise' does not appear to follow from 'no man is wise', unless men are assumed to exist. Does Aristotle assume the existence of men in this example or is he making a general statement for all cases?

17. Only indefinite nouns are given as examples, but the argument which shows that indefinite nouns are not denials (see next Commentary) may be used for indefinite verbs also.

18. The argument may be as follows. Both 'man' and 'not-man' are opposite nouns, the latter being an indefinite noun. But whereas 'man'

signifies something definite, which is a being and one, 'not-man' signifies something indefinite, which may not even be a being or one (16a30-3). For example, 'not-man' is predicable of a dog or a chair; but it is also predicable of undifferentiated matter or of something which exists potentially but which is not yet one or *actual*, or even of an impossible object, like a square with unequal diagonals, which cannot be one or a being. So since truth or falsity would apply more to what is definite than to what is indefinite or even nonexistent, other things being the same, truth would apply more, if at all, to 'man' than to 'not-man'. But truth does not apply to 'man'. Hence it would apply even less to 'not-man'. This argument, of course, is dialectical.

19. Perhaps this sameness in meaning has to be shown. We may use the following argument. If, according to 16a30-3, 'not-man' is predicable of or belongs to any being which is not a man and to any nonbeing, then the statement 'every not-man is not-just' states that 'not-just', too, is predicable of or belongs to those objects. But this is exactly what 'no not-man is just' states. For, (a) if all nonbeings and all beings which are not men are not-just, all those objects are not just, since a nonbeing which is not-just is also not just and a being other than a man which is not-just is also not just; and (b) if no not-man is just, then all beings which are not men are also not-just and all nonbeings are not-just, and so every not-man is not-just.

One may deny the truth of the statement 'every nonbeing is not-just', but the truth of that statement is posited by lines 16a30-3; for although the word 'is' in that statement gives the appearance of signifying existence, lines 16a30-3 rule out such existence as if by definition and allow other such statements (e.g., the statement 'nonbeing is nonbeing') to be true. 1030a25-6.

20. The order of words in a statement in Greek often differs from that in English. Instead of the word-sequence 'man is white', the sequence in Greek corresponds to 'is white man', and for 'white is man' the sequence in Greek corresponds to 'is man white'; and perhaps in both statements the verb in Greek corresponds to 'is white' in English.

21. 17b38-8a7.

22. Apparently, the transposition of the subject and the predicate does not change the meaning if 'B is A' instead of 'A is B' is used idiomatically or for rhetorical or poetic reasons; and such usage is proper in some languages. One may use also 'B is every X' instead of 'every X is B', where 'every X' functions like the subject 'A'. In all such cases, there seems to be no need to show by argument that the meaning of two alternative expressions is the same, for it is the same by convention. Further, since in Greek the word for 'is' in an affirmation comes first, as in 'is white man', and the word for 'not' in the corresponding denial precedes 'is', as in 'not is white man', it follows, as far as the position of the words is concerned, that the

denial of 'is man white' is 'not is man white', and this denial is given by Aristotle as the second alternative in 20b8. Then why introduce the first alternative in 20b7, as in 'not is not-man white', and argue in favor of the second alternative? Moreover, why not consider also some other alternative as a candidate instead of the first alternative, e.g., such as 'not is man not-white', which becomes in proper English 'not-white is not man'? There are difficulties here.

23. This conclusion seems to beg the question; for what has already been posited earlier is that the denial of 'A is B' is 'A is not B' and not 'B is not A'.

11

1. Perhaps man was defined as 'tame two-footed animal' by some thinkers; or else Aristotle may regard 'tame two-footed animal' as one predicate which is predicable of man. In both cases, the three-word expression would indicate one thing.

2. The word λευκόν has two senses, for it is used sometimes as an adjective, and so as a derivative word, and sometimes as a noun. Here it is used as a noun, and 'whiteness man walking' does not indicate one thing but three things in three different categories.

3. When are many things signified by one name, or when do many names signify one thing?

First, each of the expressions 'a man', 'every man', 'some men', 'Socrates', and the like is posited in 18a13-7 as signifying one thing. Thus the unity signified by 'every man' or 'all men' lies in the fact that, though the things signified may be many numerically, each of them is a man and has the same nature and so all of them have one and the same nature and the same definition, and each of them is univocally called by the same name 'a man'.

Second, if a thing is one and is definable, the name and the definition of it signify the same thing, and the name does so as a whole but the definition does so analytically in terms of elements. Thus the names in the definition, though many, signify one thing, and in virtue of such signification they are one subject or one predicate in a statement. For example, 'three-sided plane figure' is one subject or one predicate, and 'Socrates is a rational animal' is one statement and not two. Problems concerned with the nature of oneness and of definition belong to metaphysics. 17a13-5, 1015b16-7a6, 1037b8-8a35, 1045a7-b23.

Difficulties arise, however, with such expressions as (a) 'Tom and Peter are tall', (b) 'John is a tall American', (c) 'a dog and a cat are in the room', and (d) 'some white dogs are fierce'. Perhaps (a) is one statement, for 'Tom and Peter' appears to be an instance of 'some men'. On the other hand, 'some men' is not reducible to 'Tom and Peter', or to 'Tom' and 'Peter', so we seem to have two statements in (a). Statement (c) appears to have less unity than (a); for, whereas both Tom and Peter come under the same species 'man', a dog and a cat come under different species, though both come under the same genus, 'animal'; and 'some animals' is not reducible to 'a dog and a cat'. In (b), 'tall American' signifies one thing, so, although tallness is accidental to an American, still what is signified is numerically one; and perhaps similar remarks apply to (d) which, we may add, is not reducible to 'some white things are fierce' and 'some dogs are fierce'.

Perhaps the above difficulties are resolved by listing the senses of 'one'; but these problems belong to metaphysics according to Aristotle. What is clear, however, is the fact that things in different categories cannot, as subjects, be one. Whiteness is a color, a man is a substance, and walking is an action, and these three do not make up one thing. The expression 'a white man' signifies something which is numerically one, as indicated later in 20b34-5, even if whiteness is accidental to man; but 'whiteness and a man' do not signify something which is numerically one. Further, if 'A' is equivocal, the expression 'A is B' is not one statement but many, unless a specification is made as to which one of the meanings of 'A' is intended. 1015b16-7a6.

4. If the word 'a coat' means a man and also a dog, then although an affirmative answer to 'are all coats mortal?' is true, the answer is not one statement but two.

5. 169a7-21, 175b39-6a18, 181a36-b18, etc.

6. An alternative to 'as if the combination were one predicate' is 'as if the thing signified by the combined predicate were one'.

7. The reason here is obvious. If a man is good and also a shoemaker, the word 'good' is predicable of the man as a man and not as a shoemaker; but to say that he is a good shoemaker is to attribute goodness to him not as a man but as a shoemaker, for here it is his shoemaking that is stated to be good.

8. Literally, the translation should be 'said accidentally' and not 'predicable accidentally'. But here we do not have a said-of relation between the predicate and the subject (see Categories, Comm. 3 of Section 2), and no accident is said either of a subject in which it is present or of another accident. The meaning of the text, however, is clear and we have translated accordingly. Perhaps this work was written much later than the Categories.

9. The article τὸ before λευκόν and μουσικόν suggests the nouns 'paleness' and 'musicality' as an alternative, or else 'the pale' and 'the musical'; for paleness and musicality are unrelated and so the corresponding names cannot be combined. Anyway, whether we use 'musical pale' or

'musically pale' or 'the musical and the pale' or any other such combination, none of them is one predicate.

10. It is not clear from the Greek whether Aristotle is saying that paleness and musicality are not one, or that the expression 'musical pale' (or 'musically pale') is not one. Anyway, an expression is said to be one predicate if it signifies one thing, and so the unity of a predicate follows from the unity of what it signifies.

Since a man need not be pale or musical, paleness and musicality are accidental to him; but he is by definition both an animal and rational and hence a rational animal, so 'rational animal' is one predicate, and there is no duplication in it. Further, though 'three-sided' and 'polygon' are accidental predicates of figures, there are certain figures (i.e., triangles) which are species of 'figure' and of which both 'three-sided' and 'polygon' are predicable, the first as a differentia and the second as a genus; so 'three-sided polygon' signifies one thing and is therefore one predicate for certain figures.

11. Paleness is not included in man, nor man in paleness; and if a man happens to be pale by accident, paleness is then present in him as in a subject. But there is a unity, though accidental, of a subject with an attribute. And this is not the kind of accidental unity which results from the musical and the pale as attributes, for musicality is not the subject in which paleness is present, nor is paleness the subject of musicality; both musicality and paleness are accidental attributes of the same subject, of the man who is musical and pale.

Perhaps 'Socrates is a pale man' means the same thing as 'Socrates is pale', in which the predicate is 'pale' and is one; for 'man' is included in 'Socrates' and need not be stated, whereas the emphasis in the statement is on the fact that paleness is an attribute of Socrates.

12. If 'dead' and 'man' have the usual meanings, then the expression 'a dead man' literally signifies an impossible object; for by definition a man is alive and not dead, and by definition that which is dead has no life and cannot be a man. So the expression is used idiomatically, in English as well as in Greek; but another name could be used or coined, such as 'corpse' or the like.

13. For example, a polygon is defined as a many-sided figure and is said of a triangle, so 'many-sided figure' is predicable of the triangle. And since 'many-sided' is an element in the definition of a polygon and hence an essential predicate of a polygon and of any of its species, e.g., of a triangle, it is true to predicate it separately (without qualification) of a triangle.

14. Some difficult problems may be raised in lines 21a24-33. Usually, if 'A is B' is true, also 'A is' (or 'A exists') is true. But 'is' has many senses, so from the truth of 'A is B' the truth of 'A is' does not always follow, and this is so in view of the equivocation of 'is', among other things.

Now the word 'is' in the statement 'Peter is rich' is a part of the verb 'is rich', which is predicated of Peter, and it signifies a unity of two things in time, a rich Peter existing now. So the predicate here is 'is rich' and not 'is'. Further, if Peter is rich, it is also the case that he is (or that he exists), even if 'is' in 'Peter is' is used in an unqualified sense; but additional premises are needed to prove the implication. Similarly, if 'Homer is a poet' is true, 'Homer is' should be true also. But Homer did not exist in Aristotle's time; so if 'Homer is' does not follow from 'Homer is a poet', 'is a poet' does not have its literal meaning but means what 'wrote poems' means, or something of this sort.

Even if 'is' is posited to signify present time, other difficulties arise. If nonbeing is opined, it does not follow that nonbeing is; so it is not always true that A is whenever 'A is B' is true. So if the truth of 'A is' is to follow from the truth of 'A is B', some restrictions have to be placed on A or B or both or even 'is'. Thus, let 'B' be a name which is not indefinite and does not signify a relative. Then perhaps one can prove that A is if A is B. For example, let 'Peter is sick' be true; then sickness is an attribute of type B, and from 'Peter is sick' and the statements 'whatever is sick has an attribute of type B' and 'whatever has an attribute of type B exists' the true statement 'A exists' (or 'A is') follows. Even here, however, other premises are needed for the proof, and they can be supplied. The kind of B we have chosen is such as to exclude cases in which from the truth of 'A is B' the truth of 'A is' does not necessarily follow. An obvious case in which 'A is' does not follow from 'A is B' is the fact that 'A is' does not follow from 'A is not' or from 'A is possible'. Similarly, 'nonbeing is' does not follow from 'nonbeing is nonbeing'. 1030a25-6.

The word 'nonbeing' in 'nonbeing is opined' gives the appearance of signifying a thing, and 'is opined' seems to confirm this; but such is not the case. The fact that a falsity is a thought and hence a thing does not make that thought signify a thing, for it signifies a nonbeing. Perhaps 'man opines nonbeing' would be more appropriate; for here an opinion is stated to be present in a man, and opinions of nonbeing, whether they are true or false, exist in man.

Evidently, the correspondence between language and what may exist is not one-to-one, for language signifies also what does not exist or cannot exist; and in view of this noncorrespondence and the equivocation of 'is', various sophistical arguments are possible.

12

1. If the denial of 'wood is a white man' were 'wood is a not-white man' but not 'wood is not a white man', then since either an affirmation or its

124

denial is true but not both (assuming that the word 'wood' is a universal name universally taken, or else an individual), and since 'wood is a white man' is false, 'wood is a not-white man' would be true. But wood is not a not-white man, for it is not even a man.

2. Since 'man walks' and 'man is walking' do not differ in meaning, their contradictories, too, do not differ in meaning. So since the denial of 'man is walking' is 'man is not walking' and not 'not-man is walking', the denial of 'man walks' must be 'man does not walk' and not 'not-man walks'. For the verbs 'is not walking' and 'does not walk' have the same meaning. Besides, the subject of 'man does not walk' is 'man', as in the case of 'man is not walking'; but the subject of 'not-man walks' is not 'man' but 'not-man', and contradictories should have the same subject.

3. The Greek may be translated into 'it is possible to be' or 'possible to be'. We shall frequently use the shorter expression. Similarly, we shall frequently use the shorter expressions 'necessary to be', 'may be', and so on.

The part 'to be' in 'possible to be' should be taken in a wide sense. Thus specific examples of 'it is possible to be' are 'it is possible for every man to be white', 'it is possible for some men to be white', 'it is possible for Socrates to be white', and 'it is possible for Socrates to exist'. The same applies to the part 'not to be' in 'it is possible not to be'. Similar remarks may be made concerning the same parts in 'it is impossible to be', 'it may be', 'it is necessary to be', and the rest.

4. Things which have such possibility are destructible and do not always exist, and while they exist their accidental attributes are not always present in them. The word 'possibility', of course, has another meaning, and this will be considered later.

5. The word 'negation' here applies to the expression 'to be', so what is possible to be is also possible not to be. The example which follows makes this clear.

6. In other words, opposite predicates of the form 'A' and 'not A' cannot be truly asserted of the same thing at the same time. Apparently, the word 'thing' does not apply to a universal subject which is not universally taken. For if 'men are walking' and 'men are not walking' are true at the same time, the men who are walking are not the men who are not walking, and so what is signified by 'men' is not the same in the two cases, although the grammatical subject 'men' in the two corresponding statements gives the appearance of signifying the same thing.

7. In English, the expression 'not may be' makes no sense; and the correct meaning is 'cannot be'. Sometimes we shall use 'can not be' rather than 'cannot be' in order to bring out a distinction which Aristotle makes later (see Comm. 4 of Section 13).

8. In line 21b33, the word οὐ in the phrase οὐ δυνατόν should be omitted,

and the translation we give rests on this correction.

9. Linguistically, no expression in the first column of Table I which follows has the word 'not'; but all those in the second column do, for we use 'can not' instead of the English idiom 'cannot' as the negation of 'may'. The so-called additions in the columns are abbreviated, in Greek as well as in English. For example, instead of 'is possible', which is the verb in the affirmation 'to be is possible', the word 'possible' is given, and the same applies to the others; or else the expressions 'possible', 'may', and the rest should be regarded as predicates and not as verbs. It is understood, too, that the same thing must be added to two opposite assertions. For example, if 'not to be' is added to 'possible' or 'is possible', the same thing must be added to 'not possible' or 'is not possible'; and the two contradictories will then be 'possible not to be' and 'not possible not to be', i.e., 'it is possible not to be' and 'it is not possible not to be'.

10. Perhaps 'true' and 'not true' refer to statements in which possibility, necessity, what may be, and their opposites do not appear (i.e., to such statements as 'all men are white' and 'Socrates is wise', which are sometimes called 'assertoric'), or else to what such statements signify, for 'truth' means also being or fact, and 'falsity' means also nonbeing or the negation of fact.

13

1. Do the expressions 'possible to be' and 'may be' have the same meaning? According to 25a37-9, one meaning of 'may be' is the necessary; another is that which is not necessary but possible, e.g., it is not necessary that a man walk, but he has the possibility of walking (and also of not walking). According to 32a18-20, however, the principal meaning of 'may be' is that which is not necessary but which, if posited to exist, does not lead to an impossibility. As for 'possible to be', one of its meanings is the necessary, whether qualified or unqualified (19a23-6, 23a7-16), as in the case of 'may be' (32a20-1); the other is the same as that of 'may be' which is given in 25a37-9, as in the case of a man who does not necessarily walk but has the capability of walking (and also of not walking). Some logical discussion of what may be and is possible to be is given in 22b29-3a26.

Let us take the meaning of 'may be' to be that according to 32a18-20, i.e., as that which is not necessary but which, if posited to exist, does not lead to an impossibility, and the meaning of 'possible to be' as that which is not necessary but which has the possibility of being (and also of not being). Then each expression seems to follow from the other, whether immediately, demonstratively, or dialectically. For example, the statement 'some B are A' follows immediately from 'every A is B', for there can be no demonstration (see Comm. 9 of Section 7); and if one does not perceive the truth of this, whether through example or dialectical argument, nothing can be done.

First, that which may be does not necessarily exist, and the same applies to that which has the possibility of being (and also of not being); so there is no difference in the two meanings with respect to necessity. Second, that which may be is also possible to be; for if not, it would be impossible for it to be, and this consequence would contradict a part of the definition of what may be, i.e., the part 'if posited to exist, does not lead to an impossibility'. Conversely, 'may be' follows from 'possible to be', for if not, the contradictory would follow, namely, 'cannot be'. But that which cannot be has no possibility of being, and this consequence is impossible since it contradicts 'possible to be'.

The time at which a thing may be or is possible to be needs qualification. If we say that A has the possibility of being B and of not being B, e.g., that John has the possibility of walking and of not walking, we make no mention of whether A will be B or A will not be B at any time T in the future but only say that he has an attribute, namely, a power or capability with two alternatives at time T, but we deny the simultaneous existence of those alternatives at T, for otherwise the principle of contradiction would be violated. But if we say that A may be B, we posit A by hypothesis as being B at some T in the future without a resulting impossibility. Why the qualification 'in the future'? Because it is impossible to say now of A, which is not now B or which was not B earlier, that it has the possiblity of being now B or of having been earlier B; and it is likewise impossible if we use 'may be' instead of 'has the possiblity' (19a23-4, 1139b7-11). So it appears that we can truly say at T_1 that A has the possibility of being B at T_2 or may be B at T_2 if and only if T_2 is later than T_1 (18a28-9b4).

The other meaning of 'may be' in 32a20-1 and of 'possible to be' in 23a16-8 is that which is necessary to be. Perhaps the reason for this meaning is the fact that, since 'may be' and 'can not be' are contradictories and just one of them can be true at any time T, and since 'necessary to be' and 'can not be' can never be true at the same time, 'necessary to be' and 'may be' should always be true at the same time and have the same meaning; and a similar reason applies to 'necessary to be' and 'possible to be'. This reason, of course, is dialectical or sophistical. The truth will become evident as we proceed.

2. It is difficult to tell from the condensed Greek whether it is implied that also 'possible to be' follows from 'not impossible to be' and from 'not necessary to be'. Perhaps 'and conversely' is understood to apply to (b) also.

3. Whether the Table which follows was used by Aristotle's predecessors, as some commentators believe, or was put forward by Aristotle to be examined and revised, is not clear. It seems to be based partly on Table I,

for 'to be' is added to form the A's and 'not to be' to form the C's, but 'not necessary to be' is provisionally taken as following from 'possible to be' and from 'may be' and perhaps as having the same meaning, and similarly for C_4 in relation to C_1 and C_2.

4. In other words, 'impossible' follows from 'not possible' and also from 'can not', and 'not impossible' follows from 'possible' and also from 'may', and, in each case, an affirmation follows from a denial and a denial from an affirmation; for, linguistically taken, the expressions 'impossible', 'possible', and 'may' are affirmations, but the corresponding contradictories, i.e., 'not impossible', 'not possible', and 'can not' are denials. We may add, the expressions are given in an abbreviated form, for, as denials and affirmations, they should be written out as statements. Thus an explicit way of saying that 'not impossible' follows from 'possible' is to say that (a) 'it is not impossible to be' follows from 'it is possible to be' and (b) 'it is not impossible not to be' follows from 'it is possible not to be'; and similarly with the others.

In this paragraph, Aristotle points out that the first three expressions in each quadrant and their relations as stated earlier are rightly taken. It is also evident that A_1 and B_1 are contradictories, and similarly for A_2 and B_2, A_3 and B_3, C_1 and D_1, C_2 and D_2, and C_3 and D_3. Next, Aristotle will consider whether A_4, B_4, C_4, and D_4 are rightly placed.

5. The contraries are 'necessary to be' and 'necessary not to be', for these are the most different or furthest apart. They are correctly placed and follow, respectively, from 'impossible not to be' and 'impossible to be', as explained later in commentary 7. Thus 'necesary not to be' follows from each of the other B's, and 'necesary to be' follows from each of the other D's. As for each of the contradictories of these contraries, they are not placed alongside each other; for A_4 is the contradictory of D_4 but is not on the same line as D_4, and similarly for B_4 and C_4. But such placing will be examined later.

In *Aristotle's Categories and De Interpretatione* (Oxford; Clarendon Press),p. 152, lines 3-11, Ackrill is mistaken in regarding A_4 and B_4 as contraries; and because of this mistake he makes the further mistake when he says that lines 22b3-4 are misplaced.

6. Is it true that 'it is not necessary to be' follows from 'it is necessary not to be'? Perhaps Aristotle's argument here is as follows. If 'it is not necesary to be' does not follow, then its contradictory 'it is necessary to be' would follow; and such is impossible, for 'it is necessary not to be' and 'it is necessary to be' cannot be true of the same thing at the same time. But there is an opposite argument. For that which is not necessary to be is also possible not to be, and that which is possible not to be is also possible to be; so if that which is necessary not to be is not necessary to be, it would also be possible to be, and such is impossible. The solution to this paradox begins with line

22b29. See also Comm. 18.

7. Alternatives to 'amounts to the same thing' are 'has the same force', 'is equivalent to', and 'has the same meaning'; the last alternative is suggested by lines 22b8-10. The word *'reason'* indicates that the sameness in meaning of 'necessary to be' and 'impossible not to be', and of 'necessary not to be' and 'impossible to be', are taken as principles, and principles are *reasons* beyond which there are no other *reasons*. The expression 'contrary subject' here means that, if 'to be' is added as the subject of 'impossible', then 'not to be' should be added as the subject of 'necessary', but if 'not to be' is added as the subject of 'impossible', then 'to be' should be added as the subject of 'necessary'.

8. By 'in a manner which is similar' he means that what is added to them as a subject is the same for both, whether this is 'to be' or 'not to be'.

9. One of the problems concerning statements involving necessity is the proper way of stating the contradictories; and this point has been considered. The problem now is to relate these statements to the others, i.e., to place them properly in Table II and show which of them follows from the others or implies the others. Now B_4 and D_4 are correctly placed, but the positions of A_4 and C_4 lead to certain difficulties. If placing A_4, or B_4, or D_4 on the same column with the other A's leads to difficulties, then what remains is to place C_4 where A_4 stands, or better, to interchange A_4 and C_4.

10. One might object to this argument, for 'impossible to be' does not seem to follow from 'not possible to be'. The possible seems to admit of two alternatives (it may be, or it may not be), but that which is not possible does not; and that which does not admit of two alternatives may be the necessary or the impossible. Hence that which is not possible may be necessary or impossible, and 'impossible to be' would not seem to follow necessarily from 'not possible to be'. But if such is the case, neither B_3 nor B_4 would follow from B_1 or from B_2, and neither D_3 nor D_4 would follow from D_1 or from D_2. If, on the other hand, B_1 is posited as having a narrow meaning, the same as that of B_3, and likewise for A_1 and A_3, then the argument stands, provided that D_4 is so related to A_1 and to B_1, that it is inconsistent with each of them; but this inconsistency has to be shown. If the argument is allowed to stand, then, an absurdity follows. Hence D_4 does not imply A_1, and so D_4 cannot be where A_4 is.

11. In other words, if the original position of A_4 is assumed to be correct, an absurdity—indeed a contradiction—follows.

12. The possible, in this argument, is narrowed down to that which admits of two alternatives, but neither what is necessary to be, nor what is necessary not to be, admits of two alternatives; so neither of them follows from what is possible in this sense. Hence B_4 cannot be where A_4 is; and this

argument further confirms the fact that D_4 cannot be where A_4 is.

13. By elimination, it is thus shown that C_4 should replace A_4. And since B_4 and D_4 are posited as being correctly placed, it follows that A_4 should replace C_4.

14. Perhaps the parenthetical statement means this: 'not necessary not to be' follows also from 'necesary to be'; for (a) from the latter follows 'possible to be', taken universally, and (b) the contradictory of 'not necesary not to be', which is 'necessary not to be', cannot be true when 'necessary to be' is true.

15. By 'this' he means 'not necessary not to be' or C_4. Now A_1 and B_1 are contradictories; and since C_4 follows from A_1 and B_4 follows from B_1, we shall have C_4 and B_4, which are evidently contradictories, following from the contradictories A_1 and B_1, respectively.

16. Whether 'possible to be' is posited to follow from 'necessary to be' or not, something false seems to result. To avoid this paradox, the senses of 'possible to be' are considered. The assumption that either 'possible to be' or 'not possible to be' follows from 'necessary to be', of course, may be questioned; for, just as neither 'it is raining' nor 'it is not raining' follows form '5 is odd', so one might argue that neither 'possible to be' nor 'not possible to be' follows from 'necesary to be'.

17. But a man is capable of walking as well as of not walking. On the other hand, if 'it is possible for John to walk at time T' means that John is *actually* walking at T (for the expression 'possible to be' may also mean *actually* existing, as stated in 23a7-10, and if John is *actually* walking, one would not deny that it is possible for him to walk), then this statement and the statement 'it is possible for John not to walk at T' cannot be true at the same time.

18. Some things have the capability (or power) of acting, like fire, which can heat things, and like a man, who can cut things or can walk; others have the capability of being acted upon, like water, which can be heated, and like cloth, which can be cut. Of things which have the capability of acting, some have the capability of acting in one way only, but things with reason may act in contrary ways. For example, fire, when in contact with a body, can only heat but cannot cool; but a doctor can cure as well as produce disease, and a man can walk as well as stand, and he can go uphill as well as downhill. Evidently, some material things which can act in contrary ways have reason, like a man. Things which have the capability of being acted upon admit of opposites; e.g., cloth has the capability of being cut, but it may never be cut.

The distinctions above are useful in avoiding the paradox indicated in the preceding Commentary. Let 'possible to be' in Table II be taken universally to include all kinds of possibilities, even if we have the problem here of whether the various kinds of possibilities are univocally called 'possibilities' or not; for although we use the expression 'fire has the power to heat', one may regard this power as necessary since fire of necessity heats. Does 'possible to be' follow from 'necessary to be'? One kind of the possible does, as in the case of fire, but in this case 'possible not to be' does not logically follow from 'possible to be'; hence the difficulty stated in lines 22b33-6 disappears, and so does the paradox. Moreover, 'not necessary not to be' in this case is true in Table II after A_4 and C_4 are interchanged, since its denial B_4 cannot be true when 'necesary to be' is true.

If, on the other hand, the possible in 'possible to be' admits of being and also of not being, then 'possible to be' does not follow from 'necessary to be', and neither does 'not possible to be'; and in this case we have no paradox. A paradox would appear to arise if one were to assert that from 'necessary to be' either 'possible to be' or 'not possible to be', each taken universally (i.e., in all senses), must follow. Such assertion, however, would be false. For in the kind of possibility which admits of two alternatives, A_1 and C_1 follow from each other, but if so, then their contradictories B_1 and D_1 would likewise follow from each other, and such is impossible. If 'possible to be' is to be taken universally, then, although the original Table II is true for some possiblities, it is not true for all, but the corrected Table II is true for all kinds of possibilities; and perhaps such is the meaning of lines 22b26-8.

19. The word 'many' may signify more than two things; for if reason can produce contraries, it can also produce intermediates where such exist. A doctor can produce health and also disease, and he can maintain each of them; and a man can walk in more than two directions.

20. The prime movers, who are immovable, have no matter but are just *actualities*; and *as such* they act not in different ways but always in a simple and perfect way, and always in the same way (1072a19-3a13). Accordingly, they have the power of acting in this manner, but not the power of not acting in this manner; for that power can act only in one way, or else 'to have the power' here means to be acting in just one way.

21. Although those things have at the same time the possiblities of admitting opposites, they cannot admit the actualities of those opposites at the same time. For example, it is possible for John to be walking at a later time, T, and it is also possible for him not to be walking at T; but it is not possible for him to be both walking and not walking at time T.

22. For example, such are the powers to act; and whereas fire always heats when in contact, a doctor can act in contrary ways.

23. It is assumed here that he is not walking when the statement is made and that he might walk in the future.

24. Of things which *actually* exist and hence are said to be possible to be, some might not so exist, like a man who walks but might not be walking, but others are eternal, e.g., the prime movers and the Sun (for Aristotle).

25. Things which are necessary without qualification are eternal and

always in *actuality*, like the prime mover. Qualified necessity would be, for example, hypothetical necessity; and things which are necessary only in this manner are not eternal. For example, we say 'if a house exists, it is necessary for it to have been built or to have a foundation'. The construction of that house or its foundation are necessary on the hypothesis that the house exists; but the existence of that house is not eternal, and so neither is its construction or its foundation. 199b34-200b8.

26. Apparently, the word 'universal' suggests that 'possible' is regarded as a sort of genus having 'necessary' as one of its species; but one may raise the problem whether that which exists of necessity without qualification can properly or univocally be called 'possible'. One might argue that it can; for, since it exists, it has the possibility of existing. But one might also argue that it cannot; for (a) 'possible' is limited to things of which we have opinions and not *knowledge*, and such things may or may not be, or (b) 'possible' is limited to things with the capability of changing into something, whether through their own power or through that of another, and existing things insofar as they are existing are equivocally called 'possible', as stated in lines 23a6-7.

27. This statement needs much discussion; but perhaps such discussion belongs to another inquiry, to metaphysics. The names 'principle', 'prior', 'possible', 'necessary', and the like are metaphysical. 1012b34-24b36, 1045b27-52a11.

28. Clearly, eternal things are prior in time to temporal things, for they always existed; and they are also prior in perfection and in substance, as in the case of the prime mover, for He is most perfect and a first cause as mover, and without His existence temporal things cannot exist. In definition, too, *actuality* is prior to potentiality, e.g., vision is.defined in terms of seeing. 1018b9-9a14, 1049b4-1051a33.

29. These are the eternal movers, which are forms without matter, and, as forms and substances, they are indestructible. 1071b3-5a10.

30. These are substances having matter and form; and they are the physical substances, which are destructible. The expression 'prior by nature but posterior in time' needs explanation. For one thing, a man, who is a composite substance, comes into existence after his proximate mover, i.e., his father. Thus such a composite is caused by another thing which has the same form, and if that form does not exist, the composite which is produced cannot come to be.

31. Perhaps prime matter and the infinite are meant. Prime matter as such has no form but is a principle capable of receiving a form; and the infinite is in the process of becoming but without ever reaching an end. 1029a20-1, 1048a25-b17.

14

1. Why raise the question, if 'all A is B' and 'no A is B' have already been stated to be contraries in 17b20-3? Ackrill even doubts whether this Section is a part of the treatise *On Propositions*.

In saying that 'all A is B' and 'no A is B' are contraries, Aristotle is not defining contrary statements but stating a conclusion, or perhaps he is applying a definition to an instance. (1) Now a definition of contraries is required, and this is given in 23b22-3. (The various senses of 'contrary' are given in the *Metaphysics*, 1018a25-35). So one has to show that, of the various forms of statements, the two statements above differ most with regard to the same subject and hence are contraries by definition. (2) Further, statements signify objects; and since among objects, too, there are those which differ most, there is the problem of whether the statements signifying such objects are contrary or not. Both (1) and (2) are discussed in this Section; and since the definition of contrariety is borrowed from the *Metaphysics* and applied to objects which belong to this treatise, it is reasonable to conclude that Section 14 belongs to this treatise.

As for Ackrill's doubt, since the treatise here is on propositions, some of which are statements, and since statements may be contrary, it is evident that the discussion of statements which are contrary belongs to this treatise.

2. If the subject is an individual, then neither the word 'some' nor the word 'every' is needed to qualify that subject; so two statements which are contradictory are also contrary, and conversely, for the distinction between 'some A is not B' and 'no A is B' does not arise. Thus the contrary of 'Callias is just' would be 'Callias is not just', if indeed the contrary of an affirmation is the corresponding denial, but the contrary would be 'Callias is unjust', if that contrary is the corresponding affirmation with a contrary predicate.

3. If 'every A is B' is one of the contraries, then 'denial' in this discussion applies not to the contradictory of 'every A is B' but to the contrary 'no A is B'. But if 'X is B' is one of the contraries, where X is an individual, then the other contrary, which is 'X is not B', is also the contradictory of 'X is B'.

4. Universal statements which are called 'contraries' may be both false, or one of them may be true and the other false. For example both 'every man is just' and 'no man is just' are false, and 'every man is mortal' is true whereas 'no man is mortal' is false. Then why require one of them to be true? Perhaps the best way to show that the definition of contrariety applies to two statements which are called 'contrary' is to take as examples two statements which are most different and so prove or confirm the fact that they are truly called 'contrary'. If one of the statements is taken as true and the other as false, then the two statements will differ with respect to their truth-value; but if both of them are taken as false, or both as true (23b37-8), they will not differ in this respect. Of course, if the opinion here concerns

an individual, then one of the contraries, being also the contradictory, must be true.

According to one manuscript, the translation would be 'which false opinion is contrary to a true opinion', and the example which follows seems to confirm this translation.

5. This opinion, too, is false.

6. Perhaps Aristotle is thinking of statements which imply each other and amount to the same thing, like '5 is not odd' and '5 is even'; for a number which is not odd must be even, and an even number is not odd (11b39-2a9). Which of these two statements is the contrary of '5 is odd'? Now while these two statements imply each other, such implication does not arise in all cases, e.g., in the statements 'red is not just' and 'red is unjust', for the former statement is true while the latter is false. What we are seeking, then, is a universal form of statements which are contraries.

7. The two opinions are not the same in every respect; but they are the same at least with respect to being true opinions. If so, they fall short of being contrary, for if contrary opinions were both true, they would not be the most different. In other words, contrary opinions should differ with respect to truth and falsity also.

8. Perhaps a mistaken opinion (i.e., a mistake) relative to the true opinion 'every A is B' is posited to be one whose falsity arises directly from the opinion one has about A with respect to B, and there are two such mistaken opinions, 'no A is B' and 'some A are not B'; but the first would be the contrary, since it differs from 'every A is B' more than 'some A are not B' does. So since an opinion is of that which may or may not be (1039b34-40a1), if 'every A is B' is to become false and also contrary, every A must change and cease to be a B. For example, assuming that 'every man is healthy' is true, then when every man changes with respect to health, the opinion 'no man is healthy' becomes true. If the subject is an individual, e.g., Socrates, then the corresponding contrary opinions are 'Socrates is healthy' and 'Socrates is not healthy'. Such a change would be a generation, whether qualified or unqualified (225a12-7).

9. The good is called 'good' in virtue of what it is, not in virtue of what it is not, and the predicate 'not bad' does not necessarily tell us that the subject is good; for what is not bad may be neither good nor bad, just as what is not equal may be neither equal nor unequal, as in the case of a color. The word 'good', on the other hand, is a proper—in fact the most proper— predicate of the good.

10. An opinion of a thing is more true if it is an opinion of the thing than if it is an opinion of some attribute of it which does not tell us what the thing is. An opinion of the thing itself, then, would be an opinion of its nature or of a part of its nature; and the most proper opinion of it would be the opinion of all of its nature.

134

11. Just as 'the good is good' is more true than 'the good is not bad', so 'the good is not good' is more false than 'the good is bad'. In some cases it is not even possible to have false opinions such as 'the good is not bad', for 'good' and 'bad' are contraries, but not all predicates or what they signify have contraries. For example, there is no contrary to 'man', and so there is no statement which is related to 'Socrates is a man' in the way in which 'virtue is bad' is related to 'virtue is good'.

12. One of the attributes which belongs to the good is that of not being bad, and the falsity here arises in the opinion which attributes badness to the good.

13. A thing can have no more than one contrary, if it has any contrary at all. 3b24-32, 1055a3-21.

14. The contradictory opinions here are 'a good thing is good' and 'a good thing is not good', in which 'a good thing' signifies an individual.

15. Perhaps the word 'denial' would be better than 'contradictory'. Anyway, the statement 'a good thing is good', if taken universally, may be stated as 'every good thing is good'; and 'a good thing is not good', if taken universally, may be stated as 'no good thing is good'. Lines 24a3-6 indicate that the contrary opinions first discussed are about individual subjects, so 'a good thing' here signifies a subject which is an individual, as already stated.

16. If a thing is bad, it is also not good, for contraries cannot belong to the same thing at the same time; but if a thing is not good, it is not necessarily bad, for the number 5 is neither good nor bad. Hence the opinion that a thing is bad is a composite, for it implies also that the thing is not good.

17. In other words, the contrary statement should have such a form as to be applicable to all cases, i.e., it should be universal. This universality is re-enforced in the next Commentary.

18. If the contrary of 'the good is good' were 'the good is bad', what would the contrary of 'a man is a man' be? There can be none. For, whereas the good and the bad are contraries, a man is a substance and hence has no contrary (3b24-7). The name 'not-man' is not contrary to 'man'; for contraries belong to the same kind of subject and come under a single category (e.g., sickness and health belong to animals or living things and come under the category of quality); but since that which is not-man may be a quality or a quantity, it is not necessarily a substance and so 'not-man' cannot be contrary to 'man'. Accordingly, since a man is a man but one may think falsely concerning this fact, he can only think that a man is not a man. So the contrary of 'a man is a man' would be 'a man is not a man'.

19. What is similar in the first two opinions is the truth about the nature of a thing; and what is similar in the next two opinions is the falsity which denies the nature of a thing.

20. It would appear that what is not good is always bad, but this is not so. Some things which are not good are not bad, e.g., numbers are neither good nor bad; other things which are not good may be bad, e.g., bad men.

21. The word 'is' here should not be restricted to present time but should apply to any time. This is the sense in which 'is' is used in 'every man is mortal' and '9 is a square number'. The statement 'Socrates was mortal', then, would be an application of 'every man is mortal'. 34b7-18.

22. Perhaps the word in line 24b7 should be ἀπόφανσιν (= 'statement') and not ἀπόφασιν (= 'denial'); for the latter word signifies a denial, but a contrary may be an affirmation as well as a denial. I have therefore used the word 'statement'.

Is there a one-to-one correspondence between opinions and statements? If not, perhaps 'opinion' should be replaced by *'thought'*; for a *thought* corresponds to a statement or a proposition, since that which is true or false, whether of necessity or not, is a statement or a proposition if spoken, but a *thought* if one thinks about it (100b5-8). The Greek word δόξα is usually translated as 'opinion', but sometimes it is used in another sense (996b27-31, 1111b30-3); and an opinion in the usual sense is of that which is true or false, but not of necessity, like the opinion that John is sick (89a2-4, 1039b31-40a2). Perhaps δόξα here is used in a wide sense, as defined in 1111b30-3, and in this sense it means a true or false *thought* without any added qualification.

23. An alternative to 'contraries cannot belong to the same [subject] at the same time' is 'contraries concerning the same subject cannot belong to the same man at the same time'. We may explain.

If A is white and B is not white, then both 'A is white' and 'B is not white' as opinions are true and may belong to the same man at the same time; and this fact is possible, for A and B are not the same subject but are opposed with respect to whiteness. On the other hand, 'A is white' and 'A is not white' are about the same subject A; and they cannot be true at the same time nor exist as opinions at the same time in the same person, for one cannot conceive of the same subject as being white and not white at the same time.

Appendix

Aristotle, *On Propositions* 16a3-11 (tr., with notes, by John M. Crossett)

There are (A) symbols in vocal sound of what has taken place in the soul[1] and written [symbols] of [what has taken place] in vocal sound[2]. And just as letters are not the same for all [men], neither are vocal sounds the same.[3] The primary[4] [affections] which take place in the soul, however, of which these symbols are signs,[5] are the same for all, and the things[6] to which these [affections] correspond[7] are instantaneously[8] the same [for all men]. Now these [matters] have been discussed in the books *On the Soul* [and hence I shall not discuss them here], for they are [part] of another subject.[9] There is (B)[10] a thought in vocal sound in the same way[11] as there is in the soul sometimes a thought without truth or falsity, sometimes a thought to which necessarily one or the other of these [i.e., truth or falsity] instantaneously[8] belongs.

Notes

1. 'what has taken place in the soul': In Greek, one word is used. $\pi\alpha\theta\dot{\eta}\mu\alpha\tau\alpha$, i.e., what remains in the soul after it has undergone some change ($\pi\dot{\alpha}\theta\circ\varsigma$). Although often translated simply as 'emotion' or 'affection', the word $\pi\dot{\alpha}\theta\circ\varsigma$ is of wide extension: Aristotle says that geometry studies the $\pi\dot{\alpha}\theta\eta$ of magnitudes (*Metaphysics* 1355b30). Here in *On Propositions*, translators often use such words as 'impression' (i.e., mental impressions), but to do so produces problems later on, as one cannot, in English, say 'vocal impressions' in the same sense (see n.2 also).

2. '[what has taken place]': the Greek has only the definite article 'the', and the reader is left to supply the missing noun. In the *Problems*, 895a12, Aristotle (or one of his pupils) says that $\lambda\dot{\circ}\gamma\circ\varsigma$ does not convey its meanings through vocal sounds ($\phi\omega\nu\alpha\dot{\iota}$) but through the changes ($\pi\dot{\alpha}\theta\eta$: see n. 1) which the voice undergoes; and the author adds that these changes are letters ($\gamma\rho\dot{\alpha}\mu\mu\alpha\tau\alpha$). Hence a letter is a symbol of a meaningless change

which has taken place in the voice; certain groups of letters, i.e., words and sentences (τὰ γραφόμενα) are symbols of changes which have taken place in the voice and which are (a) meaningless insofar as they are merely aggregates of letters; (b) significant insofar as the spoken words are symbols for certain changes which have taken place in the soul.

The English word 'symbol' is of far wider significance than the Greek word σύμβολον.

3. 'letters' and 'vocal sounds': the Greek word for 'letters' (γράμματα) — i.e., the elements of written words — signifies (a) the letters of the alphabet; (b) by extension, literature (as in the Latin *litterae* or the English phrase 'a man of letters'). The Greek word for 'vocal sounds' (φωναί) — i.e., the elements of spoken words — signifies (a) noises made by a creature with a larynx; (b) by extension, speech, language, dialect. γράμματα can signify either spoken or written letters of the alphabet; it would appear that here Aristotle is using φωνή to include both spoken and written words (perhaps there is a parallel in Plato's *Protagoras*, 341b8).

4. 'primary': mss. differ, some reading 'primary' (adjective modifying what has taken place in the soul, i.e., παθήματα), some reading 'primarily' (adverb modifying an understood 'are'). In either case, Aristotle seems to be referring to those things which are fundamental and common to men, e.g., earth, air, water, fire, up, down, rocks, etc., which are the same for all men. And advanced civilization would have artifacts, e.g., a computer, which would not produce the same effect (πάθημα) on a savage as it produces on an educated man.

5. 'symbols' and 'signs': symbols are a kind of sign. Men speaking the same language hear the noises as symbols; men hearing others converse in a foreign language, one unknown to him, can only take what are symbols to the speakers as signs that they are speaking a language. If the foreigners begin to teach him their language, the noises become symbols as soon as he understands what they are signs of (16a26-28).

6. 'things': the Greek word πράγματα is used by Aristotle to signify actualities, whether physical (e.g., a tree) or abstract (e.g., an idea, if the idea is actually being thought or expressed).

7. 'correspond': in Greek, the word is a noun (ὁμοίωμα), usually translated 'likeness'. The English word 'likeness', although cognate with 'like' and 'liken', has a restricted significance, for it signifies an image or picture. As a result, both commentators (e.g., Ackrill) and readers have often thought Aristotle's psychology defective, since what takes place in the mind when one thinks of an abstraction is often not in the form of a picture. But Aristotle's use of the word is wider than the English 'likeness': for example, in the *Rhetoric* (1356a31), he calls rhetoric 'analogous' (ὁμοίωμα) to dialectic; in the *Nicomachean Ethics* (1160b22), he says that one can make a detailed 'correspondence' (ὁμοίωμα) between a state and a household. In

English, one may liken two abstractions (e.g., time and space, justice and equity) or one abstraction and one concrete thing (e.g., 'his will was like iron'). Where the things that affect our souls are physical, the correspondence will probably be pictorial; where they are abstractions, the correspondence will probably not be pictorial.

8. 'instantaneously': the Greek word ἤδη signifies a temporal and (by extension) a logical relationship between two events or ideas. It may always be analyzed according to the formula, 'by the time A is true, B is true'. By the time the soul begins to undergo some change — e.g., a man sees a tree — a likeness or correspondence of that tree begins to form. Aristotle will say below that some thoughts begin to be true or false as soon as (ἤδη) we begin to think them.

9. The words 'and hence I shall not discuss them here' are implied by the Greek particle μέν in the opening clause of the sentence. Such ellipses are common in language, e.g., 'I'm not going to the movies, for I have a test tomorrow', where a missing clause can easily be supplied: 'I'm going to stay home and study'.

The book referred to is *On the Soul (De Anima)*.

10. '(A)' and '(B)': in Greek, the two sentences are correlative, marked by the particles μέν and δέ. Such remote correlations are common in Greek, e.g., the μέν of 16a19 does not receive its correlative δέ until 16b6. In the sentence marked (A) and what follows, Aristotle is (a) discussing the relationship of language and psychology in the broadest possible terms; (b) emphasizing the external side of the relationship — the written and spoken symbols. In the sentence marked (B), Aristotle is (a) beginning to narrow down his topic to propositions — a process which continues until the end of ch. 4; (b) shifting his emphasis from the external to the internal — from spoken and written symbols to their content, the thought (νόημα). A thought is a species of πάθημα (see n.1).

11. 'thought in the same way': the Greek word for thought (νόημα) signifies the result of thinking; it could be translated as 'concept'.

The notion of a thought *in the voice* is at first odd, but the word 'in' has several senses (*Metaphysics* 1023a9ff.). Here the sense is that the vocal sounds are receptive of the thought as bronze is receptive of the form of a statue.

The phrase translated 'in the same way' is, in Greek, a comparison: *just as* (ὥσπερ) we have thoughts in the mind, *thus* or *so* (οὕτως) we have thoughts in the voice. The retention of both the parallel construction of the (A) and (B) sentences and this construction makes clumsy English.

Glossary

In the translation, some English terms are used in many senses or have one or more synonyms, and I have indicated this in the English-Greek Glossary. The meaning of philosophic terms in the translation are made clear in this Glossary by means of a definition or a property or a description or examples, and references are often given to the page and lines according to the Bekker text. A few terms appear sometimes in Roman and sometimes in italic letters, but the meaning is different in each case. For example, 'knowledge' and *'knowledge'* differ in meaning, and so do 'substance' and *'substance'*, as the entries for those terms in the Glossary will indicate.

In the Greek-English Glossary, English synonyms used for the same Greek term are separated by a comma; for example, the Greek word σημαίνειν is translated as 'to signify' or 'to mean', and these two synonymous expressions are separated by a comma in the Glossary. But if the English terms are separated by a semicolon, they are not synonyms, as in the case of 'denial' and 'negation', which are translations of ἀπόφασις.

English-Greek

accident   συμβεβηκός   That which may or may not be or belong to a thing; e.g., if a man is pale, palenessis accidental to him, and if he is sick, sickness is accidental to him.

according to   κατά   See 'in virtue of'.

acted upon   πάσχειν   This is one of the categories, i.e., an ultimate genus. 1b25-7, 1017a24-7.

acting,v.   ποιεῖν   This is one of the categories. 1b25-2a10.

action   πρᾶξις   Usually, an action deliberately chosen for its own sake with understanding and certainty and without hesitation. 1105a28-33.

actuality ἐνέργεια   A wide philosophical term; it includes 'action', 'form', and 'existence'. 1045b27-52all.

affected, be   πάσχειν   Synonym: 'acted upon'.

affection   πάθος   A genus of qualities which easily disappear from the subject in which they are present; e.g., a chill in a person or emotions which come and go. 9b28-10a10.

affective   παθητικός   Able to produce an affection; e.g., sweetness in sugar can produce the sensation of sweetness, and whiteness in a white thing can produce the sensation of whiteness. 9a28-b9.

affirmation   κατάφασις   A statement signifying that something belongs to something else, e.g., such forms as 'every A was B', 'some A are B', and 'A is not-B'. 17a25.

alteration   ἀλλοίωσις   Motion with respect to quality; e.g., becoming sick or changing color. 226a26-9, 270a27-30, 319b10-4.

argument   λόγος

appropriate   οἰκεῖος

assertion   φάσις   A noun or a verb, which by itself is neither true nor false but just a part of a statement; e.g., 'recovers' in 'Socrates recovers'. Synonym: 'utterance'. 16b26-9, 17a17-9.

as such   ὅπερ   With respect to size, a man may be tall, and with respect to quality, he may be sick or a mathematician; but a man *as such* (i.e., with respect to his nature or essence) is an animal or a substance but not tall or sick or a mathematician.

assumption   ὑπόληψις   *Knowledge* and opinion are species of 'assumption'. Synonym: 'belief'.

at some time   ποτέ   One of the categories. For example, to the question 'when?', an answer such as 'yesterday' or 'last year' or 'today' or 'tomorrow' signifies a specified time of an event. Synonym: 'whenness'. 1b25-2a2.

attribute, n.   συμβεβηκός   An attribute is relative to a subject, it belongs to a subject, it is not the essence or nature of the substance or a part of that nature or essence, and it may or may not be accidental to that subject. Sickness is an attribute of a man but a man may not be always sick; the concurrence of the medians of a triangle is an attribute of the triangle, and the medians of the triangle always concur.

because   διά   In 'A is C because of B', B is lthe cause of the fact that A is C. Synonym: 'through'.

being, n.   ὄν   That which exists, whether potentially or *actually*. Synonyms: 'thing', 'fact'. 1017a7-b9.

belief   ὑπόληψις   Same as 'assumption'.

belong   ὑπάρχειν   A is said to belong to B (a) if it is said of B or is present' in B or is predicable of B or exists somehow in B. For example, sickness belongs to Socrates, if he is sick, and so does man and 'man'; and the equality of the angles to two right angles belongs to a triangle. Also, (b) if A comes under B, as an individual comes under a species or a species under a genus.

body   σῶμα   (a) A three-dimensional physical or celestial object, e.g., a rock or the moon; (b) a solid, which is a three-dimensional mathematical object.

boundary   πέρας

by itself   καθ'αὐτό   For example, a noun or a verb taken by itself is not a statement, but it signifies something as a part of a statement. 1022a35-6.

by nature   φύσει   192b8-3a2, 199b14-8.

cannot   μὴ ἐνδέχεσθαι   Synonym: 'can not'. See 'may be'.

capability   δύναμις   A principle by which the subject which has it can be changed or cause a change. For example, a doctor can cure by his art of medicine, and wood has the capability of being burned. Synonym: 'potentiality'. 1019a15-20a6, 1045b32-8a24.

case   πτῶσις   For example, 'to John' and 'of John' are cases of 'John'.

category   κατηγορία   Any name which is the highest genus of things having something in common; e.g., 'quantity' or 'quality'. 1b25-7.

cause   αἴτιον   Synonym: 'reason'.   194b16-5b30,   983a24-32, 1013a24-4a25.

change   μεταβολή   In the *Categories*, perhaps the name is synonymous with 'motion'. See 'motion'.

common   κοινός   The same in genus or species or by analogy. 645b20-8.

conjunction   σύνδεσμος

continuous   συνεχές   A quantity is continuous if its parts are joined by a common boundary; and continuous quantities are infinitely divisible. 5a1-14, 227a10-7, 232b24-5, 268a6-7, 1069a5-9.

contradiction   ἀντίφασις   An affirmation and its denial, taken together. For example, 'every A is B' and 'not every A is B'; 'no A is B' and 'some A are B'; 'men are white' and 'men are not white'. Synonym: 'contradictories'. 17a33-4, b38-18a12.

contradictories   ἀντίφασις   Same as 'contradiction'.

contrary   ἐναντίον   The primary meaning is: contraries are the most different in each genus; e.g., whiteness and blackness, oddness and evenness, justice and injustice, 'every A is B' and 'no A is B'. For secondary meanings, see 1018a25-35, 1055a3-b29.

convention   συνθήκη   See *On Propositions*, Comm. 3 of Section 2.

correlative   πρός τι   If A is relative to B, B is said to be the correlative of A. Either of two correlatives is said to be the correlative of the other. See 'correlatives'.

correlatives πρός τι Two relatives which are reciprocally related to each other; e.g., double and half, knowledge and known, parent and child.

declarative sentence ἀποφαντικός λόγος A statement or a combination of statements having the property of being either true or false. Synonym: 'proposition'. 17a2-3.

decrease, n. φθίσις See *Categories*, Comm. 4 of Section 14.

definition ὁρισμός, λόγος (sometimes) An expression signifying analytically the nature or essence or whatness of a thing. For example, 'man is a rational animal' is a definition, or, 'rational animal' is the definition of man. Thus definition is used in two allied senses. 90b3-4, 94a11-4, 1031a11-4.

deliberation βούλευσις Inquiry into the means needed to bring about a desired end, usually in practical matters. 1112a18-3a2.

demonstration ἀπόδειξις A syllogism of what is necessarily true through the cause or causes. Hence the premises must be true of necessity. 71b9-18.

denial ἀπόφασις A statement signifying that something does not belong to something else, whether in the past, present, or future time, or even always and without qualification. The three forms are 'no A is B', 'not every A is B', and 'A is not B', and likewise if the time is other than the present. 17a25-6, b38-18a7.

derivative παρώνυμος A name somewhat changed in ending from the original name (with few exceptions) in order to indicate a certain difference in its meaning. Thus 'virtuous' is derived from the original name 'virtue', and it signifies a man or something with virtue. 1a12-5.

destruction φθορά Change from being to nonbeing; e.g., the death of a man, the burning of a chair, for, after the change, the man does not exist, and neither does the chair. 225a12-20, 1067b21-5.

dialectics διαλεκτική A discipline dealing effectively with any problem, whether attacking or defending or even exploring a thesis, starting from commonly accepted beliefs or premises. 100a18-b23, 101a25-8, 1004b17-26.

difference (a) διαφορά ; (b) ἑτερότης In sense (a), things which are different have a common genus; in sense (b), things which are different need not have a common genus.

differentia διαφορά If A and B are different but under the same genus, those elements in the definition of A and B which make A and B different are said to be their differentiae. For example, 'equilateral' and 'scalene' are differentiae of equilateral and scalene triangles, respectively.

diminution μείωσις Motion with respect to quantity in the direction of a lesser quantity; e.g., losing weight. 226a29-32, 241a32-b2.

discrete   διωρισμένον   To be discrete is to have ultimate constituent parts each of which is indivisible with respect to quantity. For example, three points are a discrete quantity; and so are three men, for a man as a man cannot be divided. There is no such thing as half a man; and if a man is divided at all, he is divided as a body, which is a magnitude and hence a quantity, but not as a man, which is a substance. ˈ4b20-37.

disposition   διάθεσις   As a genus, it is a relation, i.e., it is relative to a disposed thing (6b2-6); as a species, it is a quality (8b26-9a13). As a quality, (a) in the narrow sense it is easily changeable, like sickness and a chill and the like, but (b) in a wider sense it includes also habits, which are difficult to displace (9a10-3).

either of two ways   ὁπότερον ἔτυχε   For example, a man may or may not become sick tomorrow, and a statement about a future particular may come to be true or may come to be false; so there are just two alternatives.

element   στοιχεῖον

ending   πτῶσις

equality   ἰσότης   Sameness in quantity. Thus 5 and (3+2) are equal, for they have the same number of units; and the medians of an equilateral triangle are equal, for they have the same length. 1021a11-2.

equivocal   ὁμώνυμος   A and B are said to be equivocally named if the name applied to them has not the same meaning for both. Thus a man and a picture of him are equivocally named 'a man'; for the man is alive but the picture of him is not. 1a1-6.

excess   ὑπερβολή

expression, vocal   λεγόμενον   A vocal name or sentence.

fact   πρᾶγμα, ὄν,   A fact either exists or is possible, like a building 200 stories high.

faculty   δύναμις   A capability which applies to certain parts of the soul; e.g., the faculty of sensation or of thinking.

falsity   ψεῦδος   A proposition or belief signifying that something is the case, when it is not, or that something is not the case, when it is. 1011b25-7, 1051b3-5.

form   μορφή

fundamental   κύριος   P is said to be fundamental to Q if Q's existence or knowledge or action depends on that of P, but P's existence or knowledge or action, respectively, does not depend on that of Q. If P is fundamental to Q, then Q is said to be dependent on P. 2b37-3a1, 76a16-8, 123a34-6, 981b9-11, 1142b33-5.

generation   γένεσις   Change from nonbeing to being; e.g., the birth of a baby, the construction of a house. Synonyms: 'becoming', 'coming to be'. 225a12-7, 1067b21-3.

genus   γένος   In the nature or definition of a thing, the genus is that part or subject to which the addition of a differentia produces a species under that genus. For example, the genus of man is animal or 'animal', and a man may be defined as a rational animal.

good   ἀγαθός

great   μέγας   The name applies to magnitudes, not to (cardinal) numbers.

habit   ἕξις   As a genus, it is a relation, as in the case of a disposition (6b2-6); as a species, it is a quality which is difficult to displace, like bravery or intemperance or any other virtue or vice (8b26-35).

having   ἔχειν

higher degree, to a   μᾶλλον   In the main sense, if A is C to a higher degree than B is, it is so with respect to a quality. Thus if A and B are men, A may be generous to a higher degree than B (or more generous than B), and he may be darker (or more dark) than B. Some relations, too, admit a variation of degree, and so do some secondary substances. Thus A may be more similar to C than B is (6b20-7), and the species man is closer to an individual man than the genus animal is (2b7-28). Synonym: 'more'.

highest degree, in the   μάλιστα   It is the superlative corresponding to 'higher degree'. Synonym: 'most', 'highest sense'.

honor   τιμή   1101b10-2a4, 1361a27-b2.

ignorance   ἄγνοια   The contrary of 'knowledge'. One is ignorant about a thing if he has a mistaken belief about it and if knoweldge of that thing is possible.

impression   πάθημα   An affection which is the result of an agent; e.g., footprints, memories, and thoughts.

impression, mental   πάθημα ψυχῆς

impossible   ἀδύνατον   For example, it is impossible for the vertical angles to be unequal, and it is impossible for a statement to be true and false at the same time.

incapable   ἀδύνατον   That which cannot act or be acted upon.

increase, n.   αὔξησις   Motion with respect to quantity in the direction of being greater; e.g., the lengthening of an iron rod when heated. 226a29-32, 241a32-b2.

indefinite   ἀόριστος

indicate   σημαίνειν

indirectly   κατὰ συμβεβηκός   A is said to be B indirectly (or 'B' to be predicated of 'A' or of A indirectly) if A is B not in virtue of A's nature but in virtue of some one of the attributes of A, whether accidental or not. For example, John is visible indirectly as a substance, for he is visible in virtue of his color, which is an attribute of John. Synonym: 'accidental', 'in virtue of an attribute'. 418a20-4.

induction ἐπαγωγή The method of coming to know the universal through the particulars, whether these be individuals or species. 68b15-37, 105a10-9.

infinite ἄπειρον That which, though one may start going over, cannot be exhausted. For example, one may start counting the integers 1, 2, 3, etc., but there is no end to them. 204a2-7, 1066a35-b1.

in most cases ὡς ἐπὶ τὸ πολύ

insofar as ᾗ If C belongs to B but to no genus higher than B and B belongs to A, then C is said to belong to A insofar as A is B (or, C belongs to A qua B). For example, sensation belongs to a man insofar as he is an animal, mobility belongs to a bed qua a body (for bodies and only bodies can move), and infinite divisibility belongs to a straight line insofar as it is a magnitude. Synonym: 'qua'. 73b25-4a3.

intention προαίρεσις 1113a2-7.

in virtue of κατά A is said to belong to B or to C in virtue of B, if (a) A is in the whatness or nature of B or follows from the whatness or nature of B, or if (b) A is defined in terms of B and can be an attribute only of B. For example, Socrates is visible in virtue of his color, color is visible in virtue of itself, and oddness belongs to five men in virtue of their number. Synonym: 'according to', 'with respect to'. 73a27-b24, 1022a14-36.

in virtue of an attribute κατὰ συμβεβηκός See 'indirectly'.

join συνάπτειν

kind εἶδος The term 'kind' is wider than the term 'species'.

knowledge γνῶσις The name is generic; it may signify a true opinion, or a thought which is necessarily true, or an intuition or concept, or a sensation.

knowledge ἐπιστήμη This is knowledge of the causes of that which has causes and is necessarily true, whether demonstrable or not. Synonym: 'science'. 71b9-12.

less ἧττον It is the correlative of 'more', and *as such* it does not apply to quantities.

less ἔλαττον It is the correlative of 'greater', and *as such* it applies only to quantities.

lie, v. ἀνακεῖσθαι

like, adj. ὅμοιος Things are said to be like if their quality is the same. Synonym: 'similar'. 1018a15-9, 1021a11-2, 1054b3-14.

likeness ὁμοίωμα

line γραμμή A one-dimensional limited magnitude, i.e., a continuous geometrical curve of finite length. 1016b24-9, 1020a7-14.

locomotion μεταβολή κατά τόπον Motion with respect to place. 208a31-2, 226a32-3, 1069b12-3.

may be ἐνδέχεσθαι See *On Propositions*, Comm. 1 of Section 13.

mean, v. σημαίνειν See 'signify'.

mental impression πάθημα ψυχῆς

mistake ἀπάτη

moderation μεσότης An ethical virtue, which contributes to man's happiness.

more μᾶλλον See 'higher degree'.

most μάλιστα See 'highest degree'.

motion κίνησις In the *Categories*, the name is used as a genus whose species are alteration, increase, diminution, generation, destruction, and locomotion (15a13-4). In most of the other works, the name is used as a genus whose species are alteration, increase, decrease, and locomotion, thus excluding generation and destruction (225a34-b9).

name ὄνομα A name may be a noun or a verb.

natural φυσικός Synonym: 'physical'.

nature φύσις 192b8-3b21, 1014b16-5a19.

nature, by φύσει

necessary ἀναγκαῖον That which cannot be otherwise.

negate ἀναιρεῖν To negate an object is to deny its existence.

negation ἀπόφασις It is limited to nouns and verbs; e.g., 'not-man' and 'is not healthy' are negations. 12a22-5.

nonbeing μὴ ὄν The nonexistent, whether that which cannot exist, like a greatest finite integer, or that which is not actually existing but may exist, like a building 150 stories high.

nonrational ἄλογος Without the power to reason. For example, plants have no such power.

noun ὄνομα A vocal sound which is significant by convention and has no reference to time, and of which no part is significant as a separate part. 16a19-29.

noun, indefinite ἀόριστον ὄνομα 16a30-3.

number ἀριθμός A discrete quantity, i.e., a plurality measured by a unit. This is what is nowadays called 'whole number' or 'cardinal number' and is greater than 1. The Greek name ποσόν, which is closest to the meaning of the modern name 'number', is translated in this work as 'quantity'. 4b20-31, 1020a8-9, 1057a2-4, 1085b22, 1088a5-8.

numerically one ἀριθμῷ ἕν For example, 'five' and 'greater than three by two' signify numerically one species, though in two different ways, and 'Gerald Ford' and 'President of the U.S.A. in 1975' signify an individual which is numerically one.

object A being or nonbeing. We are using the name for

convenience, but there is no Greek word for it.

opinion   δόξα   A belief of what is possible to be or possible not to be. For example, 'some Americans are 115 years old' is an opinion. 89a2-3, 100b5-7, 1039b31-40a1, 1051b10-5.

opposite   ἀντικείμενον   Two corresponding opposites cannot belong to the same thing at the same time and in the same respect. The species of opposites are (a) contradictories, (b) contraries, (c) correlatives, and (d) possession and the corresponding privation. 11b16-9, 1018a20-b8.

order   τάξις

part   μόριον, μέρος   1032b12-25.

place, n.   τόπος   The first inner motionless boundary of a containing body; for example, the inner surface of a can of tomatoes. 212a20-1.

plane   ἐπίπεδον   Synonym: 'plane surface'.

poetics   ποιητική

point, n.   στιγμή

posit   τίθεσθαι

possessing   ἔχειν   It is one of the categories. 1b25-7.

possession   ἕξις

possible   δυνατόν   See *On Propositions*, Comm. 1 of Section 13.

position   θέσις

position, be in a   κεῖσθαι   It is oone of the categories. 1b25-7.

posterior   ὕστερον   Its opposite is 'prior'. See 'prior'.

potentiality   δύναμις   See 'capability'.

power   δύναμις   Capability of acting.

predicable, be   κατηγορεῖσθαι   That which is predicable of something is a name, and if 'A' is predicable of 'B' or of B, then 'B is A' is true. For example, if Socrates is a man and wise, then 'man' is predicable of Socrates or of 'Socrates', and so is 'wise', but 'stupid' is not predicable of Socrates or of 'Socrates'. 2a19-35.

predicate, n.   κατηγορία   A name which may be affirmed or denied of a subject; e.g., 'white', 'white man'.

premise   πρότασις   One of two or more statements from which a new statement, called 'conclusion', may be shown to follow.

present in   ἐν   A is said to be present in B if, not being the nature or a part of the nature of B or a material part of B, it is incapable of existing apart from B. For example, whiteness is present in a white body since it is incapable of existing apart from a body, and sickness is present in an animal or a plant. 1a24-5.

primarily   πρώτως   A thing is said to be primarily in a certain respect if it is prior to all others in that respect. See 'prior' in 14a26-b23.

principle   ἀρχή   The first object from which something either is or is generated or becomes known. 1012b34-3a23.

prior πρότερον A is said to be prior to B if (a) in time A exists before B, or if (b) A can exist without B but B cannot exist without A, or if (c) A is the cause and B the effect even if both exist at the same time, or if (d) A is better or more honorable than B, or if (e) A comes before B according to some order. 14a26-b23.

proper, adj. 'ίδιος See 'property'.

property 'ίδιον A is said to be a property of B if, not being the essence or a part of the essence of B, it belongs to B and to B alone. For example, capability of learning grammar is a property of man, equality is a property of quantity, a maximum area in a plane enclosed by a given line (i.e., a geometrical curve) is a property of a circle, and 2x as a derivative is a property of the function $x^2 + C$. 102a18-24.

proposition ἀποφαντικός λόγος See 'declarative sentence'.

qua ἦ See 'insofar as'.

qualitative ποιός Pertaining to quality. Synonym: 'such and such'.

quality ποιόν, ποιότης This is one of the categories. 8b25-11a38, 1020a33-b25.

quantity ποσόν This is a category, and the two primary kinds of quantity are numbers (which we nowadays call 'whole numbers' or 'cardinal numbers', except 1) and magnitudes (lines, surfaces, and solids). There are also secondary or indirect quantities, such as time and place, and these presuppose the primary quantities. 4b20-6a35, 1020a7-32.

reason λόγος

reason αἴτιον Synonym: 'cause'.

relation πρός τι This is a category. Two things related to each other are called 'correlatives'. Any relative or correlative may be a composite; e.g., if A is between B and C, then the pair B and C is relative to A or the correlative of A. Synonym: 'relative'. 6a36-8b24, 1020b26-1b11.

relative πρός τι See 'relation'.

rest, n. ἠρεμία The contrary of motion. See Comm. 5 of Section 14 in the *Categories*. 15b1, 221b12-4, 226b12-6, 1068b22-5.

rhetoric ῥητορική The art of persuasion.

said of, be λέγεσθαι κατά A is said of B if A is a genus or a differentia or the essence of B; e.g., animal or rational is said of man or of an individual man. 1a20-b9.

science ἐπιστήμη See *'knowledge'*.

sensation αἴσθησις Faculty of sensation; the actual sensing itself. As a relation, sensation is of the sensible; as a faculty, it is a part of the soul of an animal. 417a9-14.

sentence λόγος A significant expression having parts each of which is significant. 16b26-33.

shape   σχῆμα

sign   σημεῖον   It is a relative, and its correlative is that of which it is the sign.

signify   σημαίνειν   Signification is a relation. That which signifies is a sign or an expression, whether spoken or written, and in the soul it is an impression, while that which is signified is an object, whether a thing or a nonbeing. Synonym: 'mean'.

similar   ὅμοιος   Same as 'like'.

simple   ἁπλοῦς

simply   ἁπλῶς   See 'without qualification'.

simultaneous   ἅμα   (a) In the most fundamental sense and without qualification, P and Q are said to be simultaneous if they are generated or exist at the same time; (b) P and Q are said to be simultaneous by nature (or coordinate) if the existence of either of them implies the existence of the other and neither is the cause of the other, or if they are species arising from the same division of a given genus, like odd numbers and even numbers under the genus number. 14b24-5a7, 448b19-20.

small   μικρόν   It applies to magnitudes only.

solid   στερεόν   An immovable magnitude divisible in three dimensions and resulting after the principles of motion (physical matter and such qualities as weight and color) have been removed in thought. Its study belongs to geometry. 1004b13-5, 1016b27-8, 1077b17-30.

somewhere   ποῦ   One of the categories; e.g., in the glass, in the room.

sophistry   σοφιστική   A discipline which is concerned with what appears to be wisdom or philosophy but is not. It has as its aim honor (by appearing to be philosophy or wisdom), or money making, or just winning an argument. The last kind is called 'eristics'. 165a21-3, 171b22-34, 1004b17-9.

soul   ψυχή   The form of a physical living thing. In a man, it includes the powers of sensation, thinking, digesting, etc. 412b4-25, 414a4-14.

space   χώρα

species   εἶδος   For example, the genus of trinangles is divided into equilateral, scalene, and isosceles, and each kind of triangle is a species of that genus.

speech   λόγος

spoken expression   τὸ ἐν τῇ φωνῇ   Such expression may be a vocal name or a vocal sentence.

statement   ἀπόφανσις   A simple proposition. It may be an affirmation, e.g., 'A will be B', or a denial, e.g., 'no A is B'. 17a22-4.

straight, n., adj.   εὐθύ   A differentia or species of a line.

subject   ὑποκείμενον   A subject may be either (a) grammatical, like

'Socrates' in 'Socrates was wise', and of such a subject something is affirmed or denied, or (b) non-grammatical, like an individual man relative to animal or virtue or something which is either said of or is present in or is predicable of or is denied of that individual.

substance οὐσία This is one of the categories. 1b25-7, 2a11-4b19.

substance οὐσία The essence or form of a thing, whether the thing be a substance or not; e.g., the *substance* of a triangle is to be a three-sided plane figure, and the *substance* of a virtue is to be a certain kind of quality which is a mean between two vices (1107a5-7).

substance, primary πρώτη οὐσία This is an individual substance, like an individual tree or horse, which cannot be said of or be present in anything. 2a11-4.

substance, secondary δευτέρα οὐσία This is a species or genus which is said of a primary substance. 2a14-9.

such and such ποιός Pertaining to quality. Synonym: 'qualitative'.

surface ἐπιφάνεια A two-dimensional magnitude.

syllable συλλαβή 1456b34-7.

symbol σύμβολον

tense πτῶσις The word in Greek is limited to past and future time.

thing ὄν, πρᾶγμα Synonym: 'being', 'fact'.

think νοεῖν

think διανοεῖν To combine or separate concepts, as in the thought 'ten is greater than seven'.

this τόδε τι See Comm. 18 of Section 5 in the Categories. Synonym: *'this* individual'.

thought νόημα The result of thinking. A thought may be a concept or a *thought*. 16a9-11.

thought διάνοια The result of thinking.

thought, be δοκεῖν What is thought to be the case about a thing is what the general opinion happens to be about it, whether it is the opinion of most people or of most of the experts.

through διά Same as 'because'.

time χρόνος In the *Categories*, time is regarded as a continuous quantity, and no other specification is made concerning it. In the *Physics* and other later works (we assume the *Categories* to be an early work), the distinctions which come out of the discussion of motion and what belongs to it necessitate a number of concepts, and Aristotle chooses to use 'time' in two senses, as a number of motion, and also as something continuous but indirectly a quantity and not a quantity in the primary and fundamental sense. 217b29-224a17, 1020a7-32.

topics τοπικά Same as 'dialectics'.

truth ἀληθές A true statement (or a truth) is one which signifies a fact, whether past, present, future, or eternal; e.g., '5 is odd', 'Socrates was not a statesman'. Sometimes 'truth' signifies the fact itself. 1011b25-7, 1017a31-2, 1051b3-5.

understand εἰδέναι Usually, to know the causes. It excludes sensation, although sensation is presupposed in any universal knowledge. 184a10-4, 194b17-20, 981a21-30, 983a25-6.

unequal ἄνισος It is the contrary of 'equal'. Thus if A is unequal to B, both A and B must be quantities, and A and B do not have the same quantity.

universal καθόλου That which by its nature is predicable of or belongs to many things. See also *Categories*, Comm. 3 of Section 2, 17a39-40, 1038b11-2.

universe κόσμος

univocal συνώνυμος A and B are said to be univocally named by the name C if C has the same meaning when predicated of both A and B. For example, a horse and a dog are univocally named 'animal'. 1a6-12.

unlike ἀνόμοιος It is the contrary of 'like'. Hence if A and B are unlike, both of them are qualities.

unqualified ἁπλῶς Same as 'without qualification'.

utterance φάσις See 'assertion'.

variation of degree μᾶλλον καὶ ἧττον That which admits variation of degree is that which admits of being more or of being less, usually with respect to a quality. For example, a man may be more just or less just than another man, and so he admits a variation of degree with respect to justice, which is a quality. Synonym: 'more or less'.

verb ῥῆμα A name which includes present time and which is said about something; e.g., 'is healthy' and 'thinks' are verbs. 16b6-11.

verb, indefinite ἀόριστον ῥῆμα The negation of a verb, e.g., 'is not healthy'. 16b12-5.

verb, tense of πτῶσις ῥήματος The tense of a verb is limited to past and future time, thus excluding present time. 16b16-8.

vice κακία The contrary of 'virtue'.

virtue ἀρετή The ethical virtue is meant. As a quality, such a virtue is a habit by the use of which, barring accidents, one contributes to his happiness. 1106b36-7a7.

virtuous σπουδαῖος

vision ὄψις Faculty of seeing.

vocal sound φωνή 420b5-1a6, 535a29-b3.

with respect to κατά See 'in virtue of'.

without qualification ἁπλῶς Without any restrictions. For example, '9 is a square number' is true not just today or in Athens, but always and everywhere. Synonyms: 'unqualified', 'simply'.

writing   γράμμα

written expression   γραφόμενον

Greek-English

ἀγαθός good
ἄγνοια ignorance
ἀδύνατον impossible; incapable
αἴσθησις sensation; faculty of sensation
αἴτιον cause, *reason*
ἀληθές truth
ἀλλοίωσις alteration
ἄλογος nonrational
ἅμα simultaneous
ἀναγκαῖον necessary
ἀναιρεῖν negate
ἀνακεῖσθαι lie
ἄνισον unequal
ἀνόμοιον unlike, dissimilar
ἀντικείμενον opposite
ἀντίφασις contradiction, contradictories
ἀόριστος indefinite
ἀπάτη mistake
ἄπειρον infinity
ἁπλοῦς simple
ἁπλῶς unqualified, without qualification
ἀπόδειξις demonstration
ἀπόφανσις statement
ἀποφαντικός λόγος proposition, declarative sentence
ἀπόφασις negation; denial
ἀρετή virtue
ἀριθμός number (cardinal)
ἀριθμῷ ἕν numerically one

ἀρχή principle
αὔξησις increase
βούλευσις deliberation
γένεσις generation
γένος genus
γνῶσις knowledge
γράμμα writing
γραμμή line
γραφόμενον written expression
διά because, through
διάθεσις disposition (as genus, as species)
διαλεκτική dialectics
διάνοια *thought*
διαφορά difference; differentia
διωρισμένον discrete
δοκεῖν to be thought
δόξα opinion
δύναμις capability, potentiality; power; faculty
δυνατόν possible
εἰδέναι understand
εἶδος kind; species
ἔλαττον less (of a quantity)
ἐν present in
ἐναντίον contrary
ἐνδέχεσθαι may be
ἐνδέχεσθαι, μή cannot, can not
ἐνέργεια *actuality*
ἕξις habit; possession
ἐπαγωγή induction
ἐπίπεδον plane surface, plane

ἐπιστήμη science, *knowledge*
ἐπιφάνεια surface
ἑτερότης difference, distinction
εὐθύ straight
ἔχειν having; possessing
ᾗ qua, insofar as
ἠρεμία rest
ἧττον less (of a quality)
θέσις position
ἴδιον property, proper (adj.)
ἰσότης equality
καθ' αὑτό by itself; it virtue of one's nature
καθόλου universal
κακία vice
κατά according to, with respect to, in virtue of
κατάφασις affirmation
κατηγορεῖσθαι be predicable
κατηγορία category; predicate (n.)
κεῖσθαι be in a position
κίνησις motion
κοινόν common
κόσμος universe
κύριος fundamental
λέγεσθαι κατά said of
λεγόμενον vocal expression
λόγος sentence; speech; argument; reason; definition
μάλιστα most, in the highest degree, in the highest sense
μᾶλλον higher degree, more (of a quality)
μᾶλλον καὶ ἧττον more or less, variation of degree
μέγα great (of a magnitude)
μείωσις diminution
μέρος part
μεσότης moderation
μεταβολή change
μεταβολή κατὰ τόπον locomotion, change with respect to place
μὴ ὄν nonbeing
μικρόν small
μόριον part
μορφή *form*
νοεῖν think

νόημα thought
οἰκεῖος appropriate
ὅμοιος like, similar
ὁμοίωμα likeness
ὁμωνύμως equivocally
ὄν being, thing, fact
ὄνομα noun; name
ὄνομα ἀόριστον indefinite noun
ὅπερ *as such*
ὁπότερον ἔτυχε either of two ways
ὁρισμός definition
ὅρος boundary
οὐσία substance; *substance*
οὐσία δευτέρα secondary substance
οὐσία πρώτη primary substance
ὄψις vision
πάθημα impression
πάθημα ψυχῆς mental impression
παθητικός affective
πάθος affection
παρωνύμως derivatively
πάσχειν affected, acted upon
πέρας outer limit
ποιεῖν acting
ποιητική poetics
ποιόν quality; qualitative
ποιός qualitative, such and such
ποιότης quality
ποσόν quantity
ποτέ at some time
ποῦ somewhere
πρᾶγμα fact, thing
πρᾶξις *action*
προαίρεσις intention
πρός τι relative, relation; correlative; correlatives
πρότασις premise
πρότερον prior
πρώτως primarily
πτῶσις case; tense; ending
ῥῆμα verb
ῥῆμα ἀόριστον indefinite verb
ῥητορική rhetoric
σημαίνειν mean, signify; indicate
σημεῖον sign
σοφία wisdom
σοφιστική sophistics

σπουδαῖος virtuous
στερεόν solid (n.)
στέρησις privation
στιγμή point (n.)
στοιχεῖον element
συλλαβή syllable
συμβεβηκός accident; attribute
συμβεβηκός, κατά accidentally,
   indirectly, in virtue of an accident
   or attribute
σύμβολον symbol
συνάπτειν join
σύνδεσμος conjunction
συνεχές continuous
συνθήκη convention
συνωνύμως univocally
σχῆμα shape
σῶμα body; solid
τάξις order
τίθεσθαι posit
τιμή honor
τόδε τι this
τοιόνδε such
τοπικά topics, dialectics
τόπος place
ὑπάρχειν belong; exist
ὑπερβολή excess
ὑποκείμενον subject
ὑπόληψις belief, assumption
ὕστερον posterior
φάσις assertion, utterance
φθίσις decrease
φθορά destruction
φύσει by nature
φυσικός natural, physical
φύσις nature
φωνή vocal sound .
φωνῇ, τὸ ἐν τῇ spoken expression
χρόνος time
χώρα space
ψεῦδος falsity
ψυχή soul
ψυχῆς, πάθημα mental impression
ὡς ἐπὶ τὸ πολύ mostly, for the most
   part

Index

CPSIA information can be obtained
at www.ICGtesting.com
Printed in the USA
LVHW060518170723
752627LV00004B/251

9 781950 071043